WILDFLOWERS

OF

NORTH DAKOTA

Paul B. Kannowski

University of North Dakota Press, Grand Forks

Dedication

To Phyllis Kannowski, my wife, whose assistance on field trips was essential, and to Frances Burdick Kannowski, my mother, whose horticultural activities as park superintendent in Grand Forks first exposed me to the beauty of flowers.

Copyright © 1989 by Paul B. Kannowski

First edition, 1989

Library of Congress Cataloging-in-Publication Data

Kannowski, Paul Bruno, 1927-
  Wildflowers of North Dakota

  Bibliography: p.
  Includes indices.
    1. Wild flowers—North Dakota—Identification. 2. Wild flowers—North Dakota—Pictorial works. 3. Wild flowers—North Dakota—Geographical distribution—Maps.
  I. Title.
QK179.K36   1989   582.13′09784   89-5060
ISBN 0-9608700-3-2

Printed in Singapore

Published by the University of North Dakota Press
Grand Forks, ND 58202 USA

Publishing Consultant:
Falcon Press Publishing Co., Inc.
Helena and Billings, Montana

To order extra copies of this book, contact:
Wildflowers
Box 8238, University Station
Grand Forks, ND 58202-8238 USA
(701) 777-2199

On the cover: Brown prairie coneflower, *Ratibida columnifera* f. *pulcherrima*, Bowman County, ND, August 1987.

Contents

Frontispiece. Upland prairie wildflowers: black-eyed susan (p. 56), prairie coneflower (p. 58), white prairie clover (*Dalea candida*), purple prairie clover (p. 86), and white clover (*Melilotus alba*). Oakville Prairie, Grand Forks County, ND, July 1967.

Introduction

There is something special about wildflowers that makes them appealing, to some extent at least, to most people. Perhaps it is the intricate designs of the flowers, the shapes and sizes of the flower parts, or the delicate fragrances that some of them have. Maybe it is the diversity that one finds in a native prairie or woods during the flowering season. Possibly it is the brilliance of the colors of the wild landscape, changing as they do from week to week throughout the growing season. A patch of wildflowers provides humanity with a measure of tranquility and serenity that enriches our lives and enobles the spirit. They are part of our natural heritage, along with birds, bison, and butterflies.

I first became acquainted with wildflowers when I was a young boy. My mother was the superintendent of parks for the city of Grand Forks, North Dakota, and we lived in the superintendent's residence in Lincoln Park, a large park along the Red River. At that time the floodplain woods that were not part of the golf course were largely native and undisturbed. It was in this setting that I first encountered the nodding trilliums, jack-in-the-pulpits, bloodroots, wood violets, and other flowers characteristic of a woods in spring. As I grew older, my interest shifted to animals and I became a zoologist. However, early impressions are not readily lost, which held true about flowers for me.

Why then is a zoologist writing a book on the wildflowers of the state? There are several reasons for this. First, although each of our neighboring states has one or more books on its wildflowers, North Dakota has none. No botanist has been stimulated to undertake the task. Secondly, the research I have conducted for more than 30 years on the behavior and ecology of ants has exposed me to a substantial number of native and introduced plants in the state. Several of the photographs in this book stem from the late 1950s and early 1960s when I was involved in research on the ecological distribution and population ecology of a large aggregation of mound-building ants at Oakville Prairie, a biological field station of the University of North Dakota. Over the years I took many photographs of the flowers I encountered, in the process compiling a set of slides that formed the basis for occasional talks on the flowers of Oakville Prairie. In 1982, on reexamining that slide collection, I realized what a good start I had on illustrations of the state's flora. That summer I began occasional field trips to other parts of the state in order to find and photograph other species. By September of 1988 I had captured more than 500 species on slides.

1

This book represents some of the results of that effort. The photographs taken taken prior to 1968 were made with a Bolsey camera; those since 1968 were taken with a Nikkormat camera with a 55mm macro lens. Most photos were taken on Kodachrome film; others were on Ektachrome film. All photographs were taken in natural light.

Finding Wildflowers

The original vegetation of North Dakota was predominantly prairie, tall-grass in the east and mixed-grass in the center and west. Most of these lands, especially in the east and center, have been converted to agricultural production. Woodlands were limited mainly to the river valleys, the Turtle Mountains, and the Killdeer Mountains; large acreages of woodlands have been converted to cropland, pastures, and reservoirs. These changes have reduced the diversity of wildflowers and interrupted their distribution.

Wildflowers may still be found in all parts of the state and in all kinds of habitats. Wild, protected areas such as county, state, and national parks, national grasslands, state and federal wildlife refuges, state-owned lands, university research areas, conservation organization sanctuaries, railroad rights-of-way, ditches, and old cemeteries, as well as pastures and woodlots on private property, may contain wildflowers in considerable quantity and variety. Two useful references to some of the more important natural areas in the state are "Preliminary list of natural areas in North Dakota" by H. A. Kantrud published in *The Prairie Naturalist*, Vol. 5, No. 3, pp. 33-39, September 1973, and the special issue on natural areas of *North Dakota Outdoors*, Vol. 50, No. 8, March 1988.

Some of the principal physiographic features of North Dakota are illustrated in Fig. 1. The location of the individual counties in the state is presented in Fig. 2.

Plant Names

Each kind of organism has a scientific name by which it may be recognized worldwide. Each scientific name has three basic parts in the following sequence: 1) the name of the genus; 2) the species epithet; and 3) the name of the author of the species epithet. The first two of these parts are Latin or Latinized words, usage that goes back several hundred years when biological nomenclature began. At that time Latin was the language in which scholars wrote, regardless of their native language. Because of this practice and because a scientific name is unique to one kind of an organism, it may be recognized by scientists in all countries of the world.

The name of the genus is capitalized and italicized; the species half of the name is italicized but is not capitalized. (These two parts of the scientific name are italicized because the words are in a foreign language.) The author's name is capitalized but is not italicized. I have omitted the authors' names in the portrait section for sake of brevity. The complete scientific name of each species may be obtained by reference to *Flora of the Great Plains*, which is the authority for the scientific names used. Some species have variants

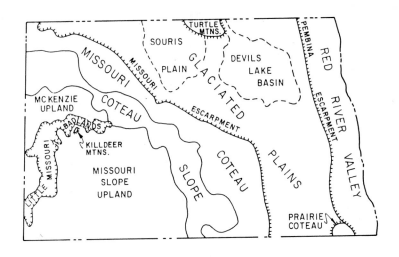

Figure 1. Principal physiographic features of North Dakota

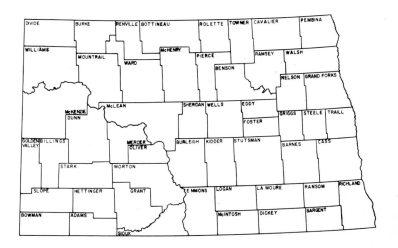

Figure 2. County outline map of North Dakota

3

(subspecies or varieties) that may be recognized by physical characteristics and that may have limited geographical distribution. A few variants are recorded in the portrait section; they may be recognized by the third italicized word in the scientific name.

Colloquial or common names are often based upon characteristics that have local application. As such, one kind of plant may have several common names and the same common name may be applied to two or more different kinds of plants. As an example, *Symphoricarpos occidentalis* is a shrub that is known by the common names, western snowberry and wolfberry. In North Dakota it is also known as buckbrush. Buckbrush is also the common name of another species of *Symphoricarpos*, which does not occur in North Dakota. Wolfberry is also the common name for a genus of plants in a different family. Sometimes the common name is derived from the generic part of the scientific name. The colloquial name aster comes directly from the genus *Aster*, anemone from the genus *Anemone*, phlox from the genus *Phlox*, and rose from the genus *Rosa*.

Plant Structure

The structural features of plants that are most useful in their identification are the flowers and leaves. Most of the terms used in the species descriptions are defined in the glossary at the end of the book. In addition, the flower structure, types of inflorescence, and leaf types, arrangements, and shapes are illustrated in Fig. 3.

Identifying North Dakota Plants

This book does not provide the means to identify the kinds of plants occurring in North Dakota. To do that, I would have to provide keys to the different families, genera, and species. That information is available in the *Handbook of North Dakota Plants* by O. A. Stevens, although the classification and many of the species names are now out of date. The recently issued *Flora of the Great Plains* is a much better source for this information. However, because this book includes species from the entire Great Plains, the keys are difficult for the non-specialist. Separating several to many species in a genus requires the use of characteristics that are seldom seen or recognized by the non-specialist.

Some species illustrated in the following pages may be safely identified from the illustrations and descriptions. Examples of these include the three red-flowered plants that are represented on pp. 72-73. Each of those plants is the only representative of its genus in the state. On the other hand, only four of the eighteen species of asters (*Aster*) and three of the twenty species of milkvetches (*Astragalus*) in the state are illustrated. Separation of these species is difficult for the specialist, to say nothing of amateurs. The species of these genera that are illustrated were chosen because they exhibited one or more characteristics that make them more readily recognized by non-specialists.

4

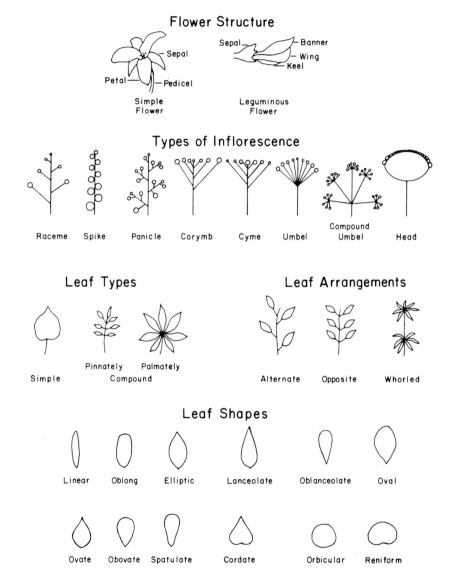

Flower Structure

Sepal · **Petal** · **Pedicel**

Simple
Flower

Sepal · **Banner** · **Wing** · **Keel**

Leguminous
Flower

Types of Inflorescence

Raceme Spike Panicle Corymb Cyme Umbel Compound Umbel Head

Leaf Types

Simple Pinnately Compound Palmately Compound

Leaf Arrangements

Alternate Opposite Whorled

Leaf Shapes

Linear Oblong Elliptic Lanceolate Oblanceolate Oval

Ovate Obovate Spatulate Cordate Orbicular Reniform

Figure 3. Flower structure, inflorescence types, and leaf types, arrangements and shapes

5

Wildflowers: Portraits and Descriptions

There are approximately 1,250 species of wildflowers known to occur in North Dakota. Included in this total are the grasses and sedges and related kinds of plants, all of which are omitted from this book. Their omission is not meant to belittle their importance; rather it is due to the necessity of limiting the number of photographs to a reasonable number. Therefore, I have elected to exclude the grasses and grass-like plants.

This book is designed to aid residents and visitors in learning about our wildflowers. There are 159 species illustrated in the photographs that follow. Two other species are shown, but not described, in the frontispiece. These are selected examples of some of the common and/or showy species.

The portraits are arranged by color beginning with white and following with yellow, red, pink, and blue. There are more white- and yellow-flowered species in the state than there are of the other colors. Red and reddish-orange colors are relatively rare. The number of portraits in each group is a partial reflection of the abundance of species in the color groups.

Flowers seldom fit neatly in color groups. The white group includes some flowers that are greenish-white or yellowish-white. I have included in this group some flowers that may occasionally be pale pink or pale blue. If the flower is more often found as pink or blue, it is in either of those groups. The transition from pink to purple is virtually a continuum. The separation here is based upon the degree of blueness. If in doubt, look in both groups. There are some green and a few brown flowers in the state, but all have been excluded from this book.

Within each group the photos are arranged in order of flowering from the earliest in spring to the latest in late summer. In several instances the sequences are slightly out of order so as to group similar species together on the page.

For each kind of flower I have given both a colloquial name and the scientific name. With the exception of several colloquial names, both names were taken from *Flora of the Great Plains*. Several kinds of plants lack colloquial names. In those instances I utilized the colloquial name for the genus.

The descriptions of the species are based primarily on information taken from *Flora of the Great Plains*. This information is in telegraphic style in order to provide as much information as possible in a limited amount of space. Information is presented in the following sequence: stem, leaves, inflorescence, flowers, and habitat. In some instances there may also be information on uses of the plant or on similar species.

To the right of the description is a map of the state on which the distributional range is marked. The ranges are based upon the maps in *Atlas of the Flora of the Great Plains*. Below the map is a bar diagram showing the approximate time of the year that flowers may be found. The final information is the name of the county and the month in which the photograph was taken.

7

White

Hood's phlox   *Phlox hoodii*

Stems compact, mat-forming, 2 to 8cm tall. Leaves opposite, linear, 4 to 10mm long and 1mm wide. Flowers solitary and terminal; petals white, forming a short tube with 5 lobes at right angles to the tube, and with a yellow throat, 3 to 5mm long and 2 to 4mm wide. One of the first flowers of spring on upland prairies and dry hillsides.

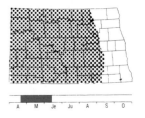

Sheridan County
April 1988

Nodding trillium   *Trillium cernuum*

Stem erect, 3 to 4dm tall. Leaves 3 in a terminal whorl, obovate, 6 to 11cm long. Flower solitary on a short peduncle and reflexed below leaves; with 3 green sepals and 3 white petals, both reflexed. Characteristic of rich, undisturbed woods, it is now relatively uncommon except locally. The word trillium refers to the three-part leaves and flowers.

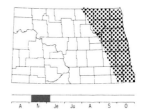

Grand Forks County
May 1988

Jack-in-the-pulpit   *Arisaema triphyllum*

Stem erect, solitary, up to 6dm tall. Leaf solitary (rarely 2 or 3), of 3 broad, ovate, pointed leaflets that are 6 to 22cm long and 5 to 14cm wide. Inflorescence a spadix that is enclosed in a spathe. Flowers small, greenish; pistillate flowers at base of spadix, staminate flowers on upper part; spathe funnel-shaped with an overhanging hood. The spadix represents the "jack" and the spathe the "pulpit." Fruit a red fleshy berry occurring in conspicuous clusters. The underground stem, a corm, was cooked and eaten by Native Americans. Common in undisturbed woods.

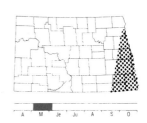

Ransom County
May 1988

8

June-berry   *Amelanchier alnifolia*

Shrub 1 to 3m tall. Leaves alternate, broadly elliptic, petiolate, longitudinally folded along midvein; margin serrate near apex. Inflorescence a 3 to 20-flowered raceme. Flowers with 5 white petals 6 to 8mm long. Fruit a globose pome, 8 to 11mm in diameter, reddish when immature, purplish at maturity. Common at edges of woods and in wooded ravines. The mature berries are edible and make tasty sauces and pies.

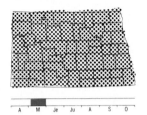

Grand Forks County
May 1988
(Fruit) Grand Forks County
June 1987

Choke cherry   *Prunus virginiana*

Shrub or small tree, 2 to 6m tall. Leaves alternate, ovate, petiolate, with serrate margins; upper surface green, lower surface grayish-green; 4 to 12cm long and 3 to 6cm wide. Inflorescence an elongated raceme of 15 to 30 flowers. Flowers with 5 white petals 3 to 4mm long. Fruit a 1-seeded drupe, globose, reddish to black. Common in open woods and wooded ravines. The fruit is edible, particularly as jelly.

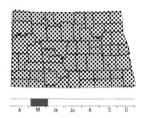

Cavalier County
May 1987
(Fruit) Bottineau County
August 1988

Highbush cranberry   *Viburnum opulus* var. *americanum*

Shrub or small tree, 1 to 3m tall. Leaves opposite, ovate, 3-lobed, palmately veined, petiolate, 6 to 12cm long and 4 to 10cm wide. Flowers in a terminal umbellike cluster 7 to 12cm wide; of 2 types: an outer sterile group with 5 large white petals and an inner fertile group with very small creamy white petals. Fruit a 1-seeded drupe, globose, reddish-orange. Locally common in moist woodland sites. The fruit is edible, particularly as jelly.

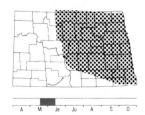

Cavalier County
May 1987
(Fruit) Bottineau County
August 1988

10

Tall white violet   *Viola canadensis* var. *rugulosa*

Stems erect, one to several from base, 2 to 4dm tall. Leaves alternate, cordate to ovate, with serrate margins and long petioles, up to 10cm wide. Flowers solitary from axils of upper leaves, with long peduncles; with 5 petals, white with yellowish base and purplish lines near base on lower 3; lateral petals bearded; back side of petals purplish tinged. Common in woods. Seven other species of violets occur in North Dakota (see p. 42 and p. 94), but this is the only white kind.

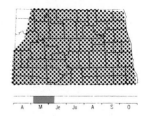

Grand Forks County
May 1988

Fleabane   *Erigeron philadelphicus*

Stem erect, seldom branched, 2 to 7dm tall. Leaves of 2 types: basal leaves are oblanceolate, petiolate, toothed, and up to 15dm long and 3cm wide; stem leaves are alternate, lanceolate, sessile, toothed. Flowering heads usually numerous in a terminal cluster; ligules white to pale pink, very numerous, 5 to 10mm long; disk yellow. Common in moist soil at edges of woods, in wet prairies and ditches, and along edges of ponds and streams.

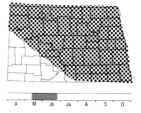

Pembina County
May 1987

Prairie chickweed   *Cerastium arvense*

Stems semi-prostrate, matted, pubescent, 5 to 30cm tall. Leaves linear to lanceolate, with 1 vein, pointed, 7 to 30mm long and 1 to 5mm wide. Inflorescence a terminal cyme of several flowers; with 5 deeply cleft, white petals 6 to 12mm long. Common on upland prairies. The name, *Cerastium*, refers to the horns on the seed capsules; *arvense* means of the fields, an apt word for a prairie species.

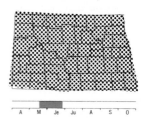

Golden Valley County
June 1983

Meadow anemone   *Anemone canadensis*

Stems erect, hairy, 2 to 6dm tall. Leaves of two types: basal leaves which are petiolate and 3- to 5-lobed with irregular teeth on lobes; and the involucral leaves which are sessile and deeply 3-lobed with irregular teeth. Flowers solitary or in a cyme, with long peduncles; with 5 white sepals; no petals. Common in woods and wet prairies. *Anemone* means windflower; the genus got its name because the flowers were found in windy places.

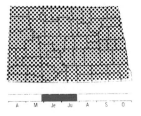

A   M   Je   Ju   A   S   O

Grand Forks County
July 1962

Spikenard   *Smilacina stellata*

Stem erect, slightly arching, 1.5 to 6dm tall. Leaves opposite, lanceolate, sessile, 4 to 12cm long and 1 to 4cm wide. Inflorescence a terminal raceme. Flowers white, with 3 sepals and 3 petals, each 4 to 7mm long. Common in woods and moist woods edges. The species word, *stellata*, means star-shaped, in reference to the arrangement of the sepals and petals.

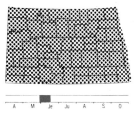

A   M   Je   Ju   A   S   O

Ransom County
May 1988

Wild lily-of-the-valley   *Maianthemum canadense*

Stem solitary, erect, 8 to 20cm tall. Leaves 2 or 3, ovate, usually sessile, with a cordate base, up to 6cm long and to 4.5cm wide. Inflorescence a raceme 1.5 to 4cm long. Flowers white, of 2 sepals and 2 petals, each 2mm long. Locally common in rich woods. *Maianthemum* is Greek for May flower. This plant is unusual for a member of the lily family in that it has flower parts in twos and fours; all others in the family have parts in threes and sixes.

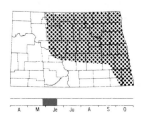

A   M   Je   Ju   A   S   O

Pembina County
June 1988

15

Tine-leaved milk-vetch   *Astragalus pectinatus*

Stems erect or spreading, branched, mat-forming, 1 to 7dm long. Leaves alternate, pinnately compound, sessile, 4 to 11cm long; with 9 to 21 linear leaflets, each 1.5 to 7cm long. Inflorescence a raceme of 7 to 30 flowers on axillary peduncles, 2 to 11cm long. Flowers yellowish-white; banner longer than wings and keel. Frequent in upland prairies and ditches. This legume concentrates selenium, which makes it poisonous to livestock.

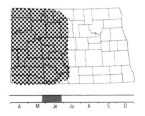

Golden Valley County
June 1983

Slender locoweed   *Oxytropis campestris* var. *gracilis*

Stemless except for flowering stalks. Leaves pinnately compound, 5 to 18cm long; with 17 to 25 opposite, linear to ovate leaflets. Inflorescence an 8- to 20-flowered raceme terminating an erect, 10 to 19cm tall, leafless scape. Flowers whitish, occasionally pink to purplish, 12 to 19mm long. Occasional on upland prairies and grassy hillsides. Locoweeds are poisonous to cattle, sheep, and horses, causing nervous disorders that make them "loco."

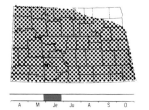

Golden Valley County
June 1983

Wild licorice   *Glycyrrhiza lepidota*

Stems erect, minutely haired, 3 to 10dm tall. Leaves alternate, pinnately compound, petiolate; with 7 to 21 lanceolate leaflets, 2 to 5cm long, glandular-dotted on undersurface. Inflorescence a many-flowered raceme on a 1 to 7cm long stalk. Flowers white to yellowish white, 10 to 14mm long. Fruit a 1 to 2cm long pod with hooked spines, readily catching on fur and clothing. Common on prairies and lakeshores, in ditches and wooded ravines. The root is edible and has a slight licorice flavor.

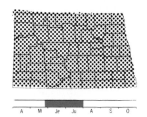

Grand Forks County
July 1982

16

White milkwort   *Polygala alba*

Stems several, erect, slender, 1 to 4dm tall. Leaves alternate, linear to oblanceolate, 1 to 2.5cm long and 1 to 2mm wide. Inflorescence a tapering, many-flowered raceme on a 3 to 8cm long stalk. Flowers white, 3 to 4mm long; sepals 5, the lateral two larger; petals tubular and 3-lobed. Locally common in upland prairie, grassy hillsides, and ditches. *Polygala* means much milk; the presence of this plant in pastures was thought to increase the yield of milk in cows.

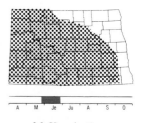

McKenzie County
June 1988

Butte candle   *Cryptantha celosioides*

Stems erect, 1 to several, stout, up to 3.5dm tall. Leaves mainly basal; basal leaves hairy, petiolate, spatulate, grayish, 2 to 5cm long and 4 to 15mm wide; stem leaves alternate, somewhat reduced upward, greenish gray. Inflorescence a cyme. Flowers 6 to 9mm wide, white with bright yellow centers. Occasional on upland prairies and badlands. This species lacks a recognized common name. I have followed Stevens (1950) in using "butte candle."

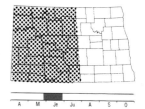

Golden Valley County
June 1983

White beardtongue   *Penstemon albidus*

Stems erect, 1 to several, 1.5 to 5dm tall. Leaves opposite and lanceolate; basal leaves petiolate, 2 to 8.5cm long and 7 to 18mm wide; stem leaves sessile, 2.5 to 6.5cm long and 7 to 19mm wide. Inflorescence a panicle, 4 to 24cm long. Flowers 16 to 20mm long, funnel-shaped, white or pale lilac with reddish lines on lower lip. Common on upland prairies, pastures, and ditches. *Penstemon* refers to the five stamens of each flower. Beardtongue refers to the tufted, sterile stamen in the throat of the flower.

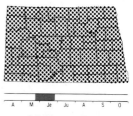

McHenry County
June 1988

18

Northern bedstraw *Galium boreale*

Stems erect, numerous, 4-angled, 2 to 7dm tall. Leaves in whorls of 4, linear, 3 to 4cm long. Inflorescence a terminal panicle. Flowers numerous, white, with 4-lobed petals, 3.5 to 7mm wide. Fruit globose, short hairy; readily catching on fur and clothes. Common in open woods, woods edges, and wooded ravines, occasional in some prairies and ditches. *Galium* comes from the Greek word for milk; the name refers to the practice of using the leaves in curdling milk to make cheese.

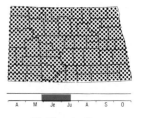

McKenzie County
June 1988

Gumbo lily *Oenothera caespitosa*

Stem short, branching, mat-forming. Leaves basal, oblanceolate, with toothed or wavy margins and long, winged petioles. Flowers solitary in leaf axils, with 4 white, shallowly notched petals 2.5 to 4cm long; flowers open in the evening and fade to a rose color and wilt within a day; fragrant. Common on buttes and badlands and on dry hillsides. One of 3 white-flowered evening primroses in North Dakota. See p. 32 for a second species. Evening primroses are pollinated by night-active insects.

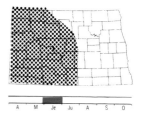

Billings County
June 1973

Pussy-toes *Antennaria parvifolia*

Stems erect, mat-forming, spreading by stolons, 5 to 15cm tall. Leaves oblanceolate, densely pubescent on both surfaces, grayish-white, 1 to 3.5cm long and 2 to 10mm wide. Flowering heads unisexual with only the pistillate flowers common; flowers white, sometimes pinkish. Common on prairies and pastures, and in ditches. One of 4 species of pussy-toes in the state; all very similar and living in similar habitats. The common name comes from the similarity of the flowers to a kitten's paws.

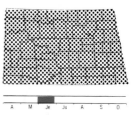

Slope County
June 1988

Easter daisy   *Townsendia exscapa*

Stem, if present, short, mat-forming. Leaves basal, lanceolate, 1 to 5cm long and 2 to 6mm wide. Flowering heads basal or on short stalks; flowers with 20 to 40 white or pale pinkish ligules that are 12 to 22mm long and 1 to 3mm wide, disk yellow. Uncommon on dry prairies and badlands. In more southern parts of the Great Plains this species may be found flowering at Easter.

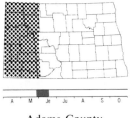

Adams County
June 1988

Field bindweed   *Convolvulus arvensis*

Stems vining, spreading on ground, forming large patches. Leaves ovate to elliptic, 1 to 10cm long and 0.3 to 6cm wide, usually hastate, petioled. Inflorescence a cyme of 2 or 3 flowers. Flowers axillary, pedicellate; sepals not covered by bracts; petals united, campanulate, white or pink-tinged, 1.2 to 2.5cm long. Common in fields, pastures, ditches, and roadsides. Introduced, now naturalized. Similar in appearance to hedge bindweed below. This is an extremely troublesome weed.

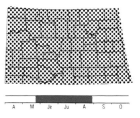

Slope County
June 1988

Hedge bindweed   *Calystegia sepium angulata*

Stems twining, climbing adjacent vegetation or growing prostrate over the ground. Leaves ovate-lanceolate, petiolate, with auricles near base, 2 to 15cm long and 1 to 9cm wide. Flowers solitary from leaf axils, on 3 to 13cm long peduncles; sepals covered by 2 large bracts; petals united, funnelform, white, sometimes tinged with pink, 4.5 to 5.8cm long. Common in the edges of woods, ravines, fencerows, and ditches. This plant is similar to field bindweed above, but it has larger leaves, bracts, and flowers.

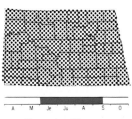

Ransom County
August 1987

Mariposa lily   *Calochortus nuttallii*

Stem erect, solitary, 2 to 5dm tall. Leaves 2 or 3, linear, 8 to 16cm long and 1 to 2mm wide, somewhat involute. Flowers usually solitary, terminal, campanulate, 5 to 8cm wide, with 3 narrow white sepals and with 3 large white petals that are yellowish at base. Petals with a large circular gland that is surrounded with hairs; sometimes there is a reddish or purplish blotch above the gland. Locally frequent on dry prairies. *Calochortus* comes from the Greek for beautiful grass, a reference to the grass-like leaves.

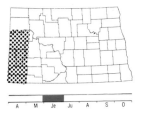

Golden Valley County
June 1984

White camass   *Zigadenus elegans*

Stems erect, stout, 1 to 7dm tall. Leaves linear, mostly basal, sheathing the stem, 1 to 3.5dm long and 2 to 10mm wide. Inflorescence an open raceme on a 3 to 6dm tall stalk. Flowers greenish-white on 1 to 3cm long pedicels; with 3 sepals and 3 petals similar in shape and color. Frequent on lowland prairies and wet meadows. A second species of *Zigadenus*, *venenosus*, the death camass, also occurs in the state. It gets its common name because the plant is poisonous to livestock.

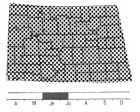

Nelson County
June 1988

Wild strawberry   *Fragaria virginiana*

Stems short-crowned, basal, spreading by stolons. Leaves basal, petiolate, with 3 leaflets; leaflets nearly sessile, elliptic, with serrate margins. Inflorescence a several-flowered cyme. Flowers 15 to 20mm wide with 5 white petals 6 to 14mm long. Fruit red, fleshy, nearly globular, 8 to 15mm long. Frequent in open woods and moist prairies. A second species, *Fragaria vesca*, the woodland strawberry, occurs in woods but evidently not on prairies. Its fruit is similar but conical in shape.

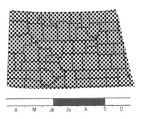

Rolette County
August 1987

25

Early meadow rue   *Thalictrum venulosum*

Stems erect, slender, hollow, 3.5 to 9.5dm tall. Leaves ternately compound with compound leaflets; basal leaves long-petiolate, upper leaves sessile or short-petiolate. Inflorescence a panicle. Flowers numerous, unisexual; without petals; with usually 4 greenish-white sepals, which fall soon after opening. Common along edges of woods, in ditches, and at edges of fens. Two other species of meadow rue occur in North Dakota.

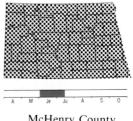

McHenry County
June 1988

Ovalleaf milkweed   *Asclepias ovalifolia*

Stems erect, slender, usually solitary, 2 to 6dm tall. Leaves opposite, somewhat ovate, short-petiolate, often pubescent underneath, 4 to 8cm long and 1 to 4.5cm wide. Inflorescence an umbellate cyme with 8 to 20 flowers. Flowers 8 to 10mm tall, with both sepals and petals greenish-white; hoods spreading, 3.8 to 5mm long, open above. Frequent on moist prairies and in ditches. Milkweeds get their common name because of the milky sap in the stems and leaves. Four other whitish-flowered milkweeds occur in North Dakota.

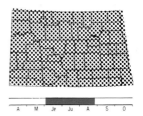

Cavalier County
June 1988

Night-flowering catchfly   *Silene noctiflora*

Stem erect, often branched, hirsute, 2.5 to 6dm tall. Leaves opposite, sessile; upper ones ovate to lanceolate, 3 to 12cm long and 0.5 to 5cm wide, acute. Inflorescence an open cyme of few flowers. Flowers up to 2cm wide, on pedicels; calyx tubular, becoming inflated, 15 to 30mm long, with 10 green nerves, hirsute; petals 5, white to pinkish, deeply cleft, spreading at right angles from the tubular base. An introduced weed, now naturalized. Common in fields, ditches, and gardens.

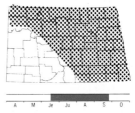

Bottineau County
August 1988

26

27

Cow parsnip   *Heracleum sphondylium montanum*

Stems erect, stout, densely pubescent, grooved, up to 3m tall. Leaves ternate, 2.5dm long and wide, petiolate; leaflets lobed with toothed margins. Inflorescence a compound umbel. Flowers 2mm wide, white. Fruit obovate, flattened with lateral wings, 8 to 12mm long and 6 to 9mm wide. Common in woods and moist woods edges. The foliage may cause dermatitis in humans. Similar species that occur in the state include *Cicuta maculata*, water hemlock, and *Conium maculatum*, poison hemlock; all parts of the latter are poisonous.

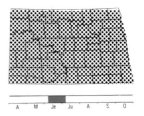

Bottineau County
June 1987

Tall cinquefoil   *Potentilla arguta*

Stems erect, solitary, densely hairy, 3 to 10dm tall. Leaves of 2 types; basal leaves petiolate, pinnately compound with 7 to 9 leaflets increasing in size to the apex; stem leaves short-petioled or sessile, with fewer and smaller leaflets. Inflorescence cymose. Flowers 12 to 15mm wide, with 5 white petals. Frequent on moist prairies and in ditches. Most cinquefoils have yellow flowers, one of which is illustrated on p. 50. Cinquefoil refers to 5-parted leaves, a characteristic of some species of *Potentilla*, but not this one.

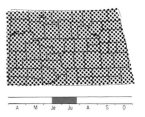

McHenry County
June 1987

Meadow-sweet   *Spirea alba*

Shrubs up to 1.2m tall, with reddish stems. Leaves alternate, petiolate, oblanceolate, with serrate margins, 3 to 6cm long and 1 to 2cm wide. Inflorescence an elongate, terminal panicle of numerous small flowers. Flowers 5 to 8mm wide with 5 white petals. Locally abundant in moist prairies and sandhills. The root has been used for food.

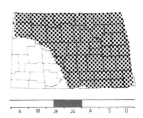

Ransom County
July 1988

Yucca *Yucca glauca*

Stems short, basal. Leaves basal, linear, stiff, sharp-pointed, 4 to 7dm long and 5 to 15mm wide; evergreen and perennial. Inflorescence an elongate raceme extending well above the leaves. Flowers large and campanulate, with 3 sepals and 3 petals similar in shape and size, greenish white. Common on upland prairies and badlands, especially on grassy hillsides. Parts of the plant were useful to Native Americans: fruit and petals as food, roots for soap, and leaf fibers for sewing.

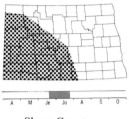

Slope County
June 1984

Palespike lobelia *Lobelia spicata*

Stems erect, slender, usually unbranched, 3 to 10dm tall. Leaves oblanceolate, 2 to 6cm long and 0.5 to 2cm wide. Inflorescence a loose, elongate, terminal raceme. Flowers bluish-white to white, 7 to 13mm long; petals tubular, forming 2 lips, an upper lip of 2 small lobes and a lower lip of 3 larger lobes. Frequent in lowland prairies and moist ditches.

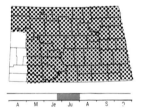

Grand Forks County
June 1988

Wintergreen *Pyrola elliptica*

Plant without stem. Leaves 3 to 7, basal, oval, petiolate, 2 to 7cm long; evergreen. Inflorescence a raceme of 8 to 13 flowers on a 1 to 2.5dm tall stalk. Flowers 1 to 1.2cm across on 3 to 7mm long pedicels; with 5 petals 6 to 8mm long, white to greenish-white, reflexed. Uncommon in rich, moist woods. Two other species of wintergreen occur in North Dakota in the same habitat.

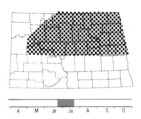

Bottineau County
June 1988

Wild buckwheat   *Polygonum convolvulus*

Twining vine with rough stems, 1m or more
in length. Leaves cordate, petiolate,
pointed, up to 6cm long and 5cm wide. Inflorescence a raceme, terminal and axillary
in upper leaves. Flowers with sepals but no
petals, greenish-white, angular, 5-lobed, 1
to 2mm long. Common in edges of woods,
fencerows, and ditches.

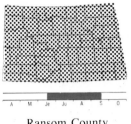

Ransom County
August 1987

White-stemmed evening primrose   *Oenothera nuttallii*

Stems erect, branched, white, with exfoliating epidermis, 3 to 6dm tall. Leaves
alternate, linear to lanceolate, sessile or
short-petioled, 2 to 6cm long and 3 to 7mm
wide. Flowers solitary, axillary with 4
obovate, white petals 1.5 to 2.5cm long;
petals becoming pinkish on fading. Locally common in sandhills, dry upland
prairies, and roadsides. The flowers usually
open in the evening and last only a day.
The pale evening primrose (*Oenothera
albicaulis*) has similar flowers but the leaves
are deeply pinnately-cleft.

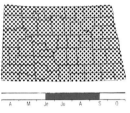

Bowman County
August 1988

Prairie larkspur   *Delphinium virescens*

Stems erect, sturdy, sometimes branched,
pubescent, 5 to 12dm tall. Leaves basal and
alternate along stem; lowest leaves long-
petioled, petioles reduced upward;
palmately divided into 3 to 7 main lobes.
Inflorescence terminal, elongate, spikelike
raceme of 5 to 30 flowers. Flowers with 5
petal-like sepals and 4 petals, whitish; uppermost sepal with a spur 11 to 20mm long;
lower 2 petals bifid and bearded. Occasional on lowland prairies and in moist
ditches. This plant is poisonous to livestock.

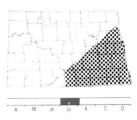

Griggs County
July 1982

32

Arrowhead *Sagittaria cuneata*

Aquatic or semiaquatic plant. Leaves arrow-shaped and long-petioled; leaf blades 5 to 15cm long; petioles angular. Inflorescence few-flowered in whorls of 3, lower flowers usually pistillate and upper ones staminate. Flowers 1 to 2.5cm wide, with 3 white petals; staminate flowers with yellow centers. Fruiting heads globose. Frequent in shallow ponds and along lake and stream shores. Another species (*Sagittaria latifolia*) occurs in the same habitats and is very similar. Underground stems, called duck potatoes, are edible when cooked.

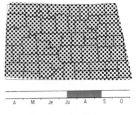

Bottineau County
August 1988

Lady's-tresses *Spiranthes cernua*

Stems erect, usually solitary, up to 60cm tall. Leaves mainly basal, linear to lanceolate, up to 25cm long and 2.5cm wide. Flowers in a dense spike, usually in spirally-arranged rows totaling up to 60 flowers, white with a yellowish-green center on the lip. Occasional in moist prairie and fens. Two other species of lady's-tresses may be found in similar habitats in the state.

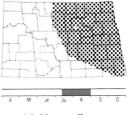

McHenry County
July 1987

Prickly poppy *Argemone polyanthemos*

Stems erect, usually branched, sparingly prickly, 4 to 15cm tall, with yellow sap. Leaves oblanceolate with winged petiole; deeply pinnately lobed with undulate and spiny margins; 7 to 20cm long and 3 to 10cm wide; upper leaves reduced in size and usually sessile. Flowers on 1 to 4cm long peduncles; 5 to 10cm wide; with 3 sepals and 6 white petals. Introduced, possibly as an escape from cultivation. The specimen pictured was found in sandy soil of a pasture.

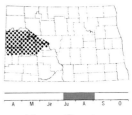

Mercer County
July 1981

Indian pipe   *Monotropa uniflora*

Saprophytic or parasitic plants without chlorophyl. Stems erect, fleshy, unbranched, off-white to pink, 7 to 30cm tall. Leaves absent, replaced by scales that are sessile, lanceolate, ascending, and 6 to 12mm long. Flowers solitary, terminal, nodding but becoming upright at maturity, 1.4 to 3cm long; often without sepals; with 5 oblong petals, off-white to pink. Entire plant becomes blackened upon drying. Known only from dense hardwoods. *Monotropa* refers to the occurrence of single flowers on the stem.

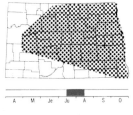

Dunn County
July 1976

Aster   *Aster lucidulus*

Stems erect, slender, more or less ribbed, 4 to 25dm tall. Leaves lanceolate to ovate-lanceolate, sessile, clasping, 4 to 7cm long and 1 to 2.5cm wide. Inflorescence of several heads in an open, paniculate cluster with up to 100 heads. Flowering heads with 30 to 40 ray ligules, each 10 to 14mm long, white to bluish; disk yellow. Frequent in fens and other marshy ground. Two other species of white-flowered asters are presented below and on p. 40. A blue-flowered species is described on p. 112.

Mountrail County
August 1988

Panicled aster   *Aster simplex*

Stems erect, solitary or several, stout, branched, 6 to 15dm tall. Leaves linear to lanceolate, sessile or subsessile, 7 to 15cm long and 3 to 35mm wide, reduced in size upwards. Inflorescence of many heads in an open, paniculate cluster. Flowering heads with 25 to 35 ray ligules, each 4 to 7mm long, white, occasionally pink or lavender. Moist prairies and woods edges.

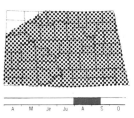

Rolette County
August 1987

36

Sneezewort aster   *Solidago ptarmicoides*

Stems erect, clustered, 1 to 7dm tall. Leaves at base linear-lanceolate, petiolate, 3 to 20cm long and 3 to 10mm wide; stem leaves reduced upward. Inflorescence an open, flat-topped corymb with 3 to 60 heads. Flowering heads with 10 to 25 white ligules, each 5 to 9mm long; disk white. Frequent on prairies and in ditches. The only white-flowered member of the goldenrod genus, *Solidago*, this species was formerly classified in the genus *Aster*, the members of which it greatly resembles.

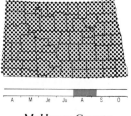

McHenry County
August 1988

False boneset   *Kuhnia eupatorioides*

Stems erect, densely pubescent, 3 to 10dm tall. Leaves numerous, occurring only on the stem, lanceolate, usually toothed, 2 to 10cm long and 0.5 to 4cm wide. Inflorescence a small corymbiform cluster at end of a branch. Flowering heads formed of disk florets only; with 7 to 35 creamy-white florets. Upland prairie and ditches.

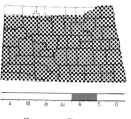

Sargent County
August 1987

White lettuce   *Prenanthes alba*

Stems erect, smooth, with milky sap, 5 to 15dm tall. Leaves alternate on stem; lower ones petiolate, lobed, toothed; upper ones smaller, less lobed, and less petiolate. Inflorescence like a panicle, elongate, representing the upper 1/4 to 1/3 of the plant. Flowering heads nodding, with usually 9 ligulate florets; ligules white to pale pink. Locally frequent in open woods and woods edges. One additional species of *Prenanthes* occurs in the state; it has bluish flowers and occurs on prairies.

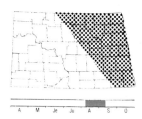

Ransom County
August 1982

38

39

Annual eriogonum   *Eriogonum annuum*

Stems erect, solitary or branched upwards, densely pubescent, grayish, 1 to 10dm tall. Leaves alternate, oblanceolate, 2 to 5cm long, numerous on lower portion of stem, few elsewhere. Inflorescence terminal, open-cymose, 1 to 1.5dm wide. Flowers numerous and white, often tinged with pink. A striking plant that is locally common in sandhills and sandy upland prairies.

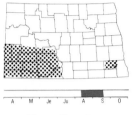

Slope County
August 1987

Aster   *Aster pansus*

Stems erect, branched, tufted, 3 to 10dm tall. Leaves alternate; lower ones early deciduous, upper stem leaves persistent; linear, 1 to 5cm long and up to 3mm wide. Inflorescence of numerous small heads. Heads with 10 to 18 ray ligules, white, less than 6mm long; disk yellow. Frequent on upland prairies, in ditches and along roadsides. Three other species of white, small-flowered asters occur in North Dakota, the commonest being *Aster ericoides*, which has an open, branched growth form.

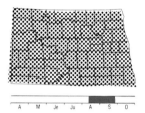

Slope County
August 1988

Boneset   *Eupatorium perfoliatum*

Stems erect, conspicuously hairy, 4 to 15dm tall. Leaves opposite, with bases united around the stem, with toothed margins, 7 to 20cm long and up to 4cm wide. Inflorescence a modified, flat-topped cyme. Heads with 9 to 23 ray florets, white; without disk florets. Common in open, damp sites in extreme southeastern North Dakota.

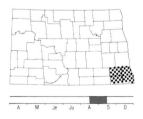

Ransom County
August 1987

40

41

Yellow

Downy yellow violet   *Viola pubescens*

Stems erect or spreading, 1 to 4dm tall. Leaves broadly ovate, with toothed margins, long petioled, mostly basal; with 2 to 4 stem leaves located near top. Flowers solitary in leaf axils; petals 5, yellow, lower 3 with dark veins, lateral 2 bearded. The stems, leaves and peduncles are often pubescent, hence "downy." Commonly found in woods. The only other yellow violet in the state is the yellow prairie violet, *Viola nuttallii*, which occurs on prairies.

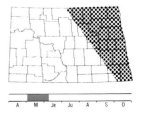

Grand Forks County
May 1988

Marsh marigold   *Caltha palustris*

Stems erect, 2 to 6dm tall, hollow. Leaves basal and alternate, long petioled (8 to 30cm), nearly circular with toothed or scalloped margins, 3 to 10cm long by 4 to 15cm wide. Flowers axillary or terminal, 2 to 5cm wide, with 5 or 6 yellow sepals, no petals. Locally common in marshes and wet meadows. The species epithet, *palustris*, means of the marshes.

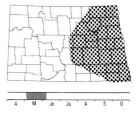

Ransom County
May 1988

Prairie buck bean   *Thermopsis rhombifolia*

Stems erect, often branched, 1.5 to 4dm tall. Leaves alternate, palmately trifoliate; leaflets lanceolate, 1.5 to 3cm long and 1 to 2cm wide, pubescent. Inflorescence subterminal axillary racemes, up to 1dm long, with 10 to 30 flowers. Flowers golden yellow, 1.5 to 2cm long, consisting of 4 parts: upper banner, 2 lateral wings, and the lower keel representing two fused petals. Frequent on upland prairies and badlands.

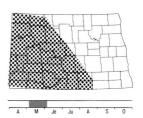

Billings County
May 1972

Golden alexanders   *Zizia aptera*

Stem erect, 3 to 7dm tall. Basal leaves usually cordate with toothed margins and 5 to 10cm long petioles; stem leaves divided into 3 lanceolate segments with serrate edges. Inflorescence of compound umbels, 3 to 5cm wide. Flowers yellow. Very common in wet meadows. A related species, *Zizia aurea*, has ternate basal leaves; it occurs in moist sites in woods.

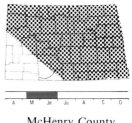

McHenry County
June 1988

Bristly buttercup   *Ranunculus hispidus* var. *caricetorum*

Stems erect or creeping, 1.5 to 7dm tall. Basal leaves with 0.5 to 3dm long petioles, ternate or 3-lobed, blades 3-14cm long by 3 to 20cm wide; stem leaves shorter petioled upwards. Flowers terminal, showy; petals 5, yellow, with a waxy patina, 7 to 16mm long. Common in wet meadows. There are more than a dozen other species of yellow-flowered buttercups in North Dakota. See also the threadleaf buttercup on p. 56. *Ranunculus* means little frog, so named because many buttercups occur in marshy areas where frogs also occur.

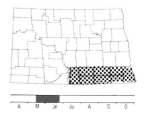

Ransom County
May 1988

Yellow wild buckwheat   *Eriogonum flavum*

Stem short, spreading. Leaves petioled, 3 to 8cm long, 3 to 14mm wide, petioled, rather thick, greenish above, grayish underneath. Inflorescence an umbel, 2 to 5cm wide on a 4 to 25cm long stem subtended by from 4 to 6 leaflike bracts. Flowers yellow. Common in upland prairie and badlands.

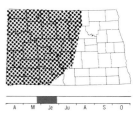

Williams County
May 1985

44

False dandelion   *Agoseris glauca*

Stems leafless, bearing flowers, 1 to 3dm tall. Leaves basal in rosette, lanceolate, often with toothed margins, 5 to 30cm long, 1 to 30mm wide. Flowering heads solitary at ends of stems, 2 to 5cm wide, yellow, formed of ray florets only. Stems and leaves have a milky sap. Common in prairies and ditches, especially in moist sites. Native Americans chewed the hardened sap of this plant.

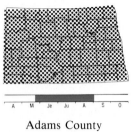

Adams County
June 1988

Stemless hymenoxys   *Hymenoxys acaulis*

Stems leafless, bearing flowers, 1 to 3dm tall. Leaves basal in rosette, linear lanceolate, margins entire, 2 to 6cm long, up to 8mm wide. Flowering heads solitary at ends of stems, 2 to 4cm wide, yellow, with 8 to 13 ligules typically 3-pointed at distal end. Upland prairies and badlands.

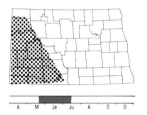

Golden Valley County
June 1983

Goat's beard   *Tragopogon dubius*

Stems erect, smooth, usually branched, 3 to 8dm tall, containing a milky sap. Leaves alternate, long-linear, tapering to apex, up to 30cm long. Flowering heads solitary at the ends of stalks, which are swollen below the heads; of ray florets only; yellow; with 8 to 13 long slender bracts that exceed the florets. Fruiting head like a giant dandelion "ball." An introduced weed that is common in ditches and disturbed sites. The root is edible.

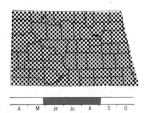

Barnes County
May 1988

(Fruit) Griggs County
July 1982

46

Western wallflower   *Erysimum asperum*

Stems erect, stiff, usually branched, 2 to 10dm tall. Leaves numerous, linear to lanceolate, margins sometimes toothed, 3 to 8cm long, ends curving downward. Inflorescence a raceme. Flowers showy; petals 4, golden yellow, 15 to 25mm long. Fruits stiffly spreading, 4-angled pods, 8 to 12cm long. Common and conspicuous on prairies and in ditches.

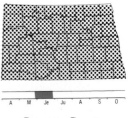

Ransom County
May 1988

Plains yellow primrose   *Calylophus serrulatus*

Stems erect or decumbent, usually branched, 0.5 to 8dm tall. Leaves alternate, linear to lanceolate, with finely serrate margins, 1 to 10cm long and 1 to 12mm wide. Flowers borne in axils of upper leaves; petals 4, 5 to 14mm long and about as wide, yellow. Fruit a dehiscent capsule, 1 to 3cm long and 1 to 3mm wide. A common plant of prairies and badlands, also often in ditches. Resembles evening primroses, to which it is closely related; however, this plant blooms in the daytime.

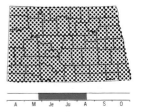

Golden Valley County
June 1984

Gray ragwort   *Senecio canus*

Stems usually solitary, erect, gray due to dense pubescence, 1 to 3dm tall. Basal leaves petiolate, ovate to lanceolate, 2.5 to 5cm long and 1 to 3cm wide; stem leaves reduced in size upward. Inflorescence a cyme of 6 to 12 heads. Flowers yellow, with both disk and ray florets; ligules 7 to 10mm long. Upland prairies and grassy badlands sites. Eight other kinds of ragworts are known to occur in North Dakota.

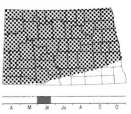

Golden Valley County
June 1983

48

Yellow lady's-slipper   *Cypripedium calceolus*

Stems erect, leafy, 2 to 3dm tall. Leaves 3 to 6, alternate, ovate-lanceolate, plicate, 5 to 21cm long and 2 to 11cm wide. Flowers 1 or 2 per stem, with sepals and lateral petals greenish to yellowish brown; the petals spirally twisted; the lower petal, the lip (= the slipper), saclike, 1.8 to 5cm long. Occasional in moist sites in woods, along streams, and in ditches. There are 3 other species of lady's-slippers in the Great Plains, and all 3 occur, albeit rarely, in North Dakota.

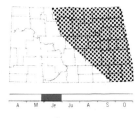

Cavalier County
May 1987

Silverweed   *Potentilla anserina*

Stems creeping, forming runners that root at the nodes. Leaves lanceolate, pinnately compound, usually greenish above and whitish below, 1 to 3dm long; leaflets sharply toothed. Flowers solitary on erect peduncles; petals 5, yellow, 6 to 12mm long. Frequent in wet meadows and ditches, especially on saline soils. The roots are edible. Thirteen other species of *Potentilla* occur in North Dakota.

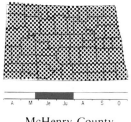

McHenry County
June 1988

Gromwell   *Lithospermum incisum*

Stems erect, often branched, up to 4dm tall. Leaves usually only on stems, linear, pubescent, 1.3 to 4.5cm long and 4 to 10mm wide. Inflorescence a terminal cyme. Flowers with petals united into a long tube with 5 lobes, the margins of which are ruffled and toothed; pale to golden yellow. Common on upland prairie and in dry sites in ditches. Another species of *Lithospermum* (*canescens*), hoary puccoon, is common on our prairies; its flowers are orangish.

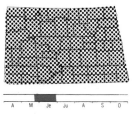

Stutsman County
June 1982

50

51

Downy paintbrush   *Castilleja sessiliflora*

Stems erect, 1 to 3dm tall, often clustered. Leaves alternate, sessile, linear, 2 to 5cm long. Inflorescence a spike. Flowers yellowish to purple, 3.5 to 5.5cm long, slender, partially surrounded by greenish or pink-tipped bracts. This conspicuous little plant is occasionally common on upland prairies and in badlands. It is the only species of paintbrush to occur in the state. The colors of paintbrush are due to the bracts rather than the flowers, which are small and partially hidden.

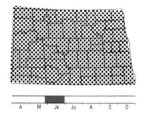

Golden Valley County
June 1983

Blanket flower   *Gaillardia aristata*

Stems single or clustered, densely hirsute, 3 to 6dm tall. Leaves alternate on stem, oblong to lanceolate, entire to deeply lobed. Flowers solitary or several on long stalks, 3 to 6cm wide; ray ligules 1 to 3cm long, yellow, sometimes reddish-purple near disk; disk reddish-purple, dome-shaped. Common on upland prairies and in dry sites in ditches.

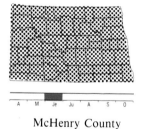

McHenry County
June 1987

Yellow wood sorrel   *Oxalis stricta*

Stems erect or spreading, up to 4dm tall, densely pubescent. Leaves alternate, petiolate, compound with 3 cordate leaflets; leaflets folding together at night. Inflorescence 1-flowered. Flowers with 5 petals, bright yellow. Frequent in woods, fields and disturbed sites. *Oxalis* is derived from the Greek word for sharp, a reference to the sharp taste of the leaves, which contain oxalic acid.

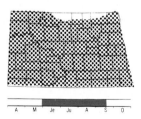

Ransom County
August 1987

52

53

Solomon's seal   *Polygonatum biflorum*

Stem solitary, erect, usually arching to one side, 6 to 12dm tall. Leaves alternate, ovate-lanceolate, sessile, 7 to 16cm long and 3 to 9cm wide. Inflorescence axillary with 2 or 3 flowers hanging down at each axil. Flowers greenish white to cream colored, united into a cylindrical tube with 6 lobes. Fruit a dark blue berry. Common in woods.

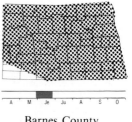

Barnes County
June 1987

Plains prickly pear   *Opuntia polyacantha*

Stem prostrate, clumped; stem segments greenish-gray, bilaterally compressed, orbicular to ovate; areoles bearing 1 to 10 long, straight spines and several smaller spines. No leaves. Flowers 4 to 7cm wide, with many yellow petals. Fruit globose, reddish; edible. Common on upland prairies and badlands. One other species of prickly pear, little prickly pear (*Opuntia fragilis*), occurs in the state. It has smaller and fewer segments, which separate readily. It seldom produces flowers.

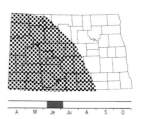

Burleigh County
June 1982

Hawk's-beard   *Crepis tectorum*

Stem erect, branched, 2 to 4dm tall. Leaves on stems sessile, clasping, lanceolate to linear; basal leaves lanceolate with a winged petiole, early deciduous. Inflorescence a branching cluster of few to many heads. Flowers yellow, of only ray florets, about 13mm wide. Introduced weed in fields and ditches in a few widely scattered localities.

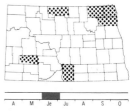

Pembina County
June 1988

54

55

Threadleaf buttercup   *Ranunculus flabellaris*

Stems floating in water or erect on moist ground, branched. Leaves on stems; lower ones long petioled, upper ones subsessile; blades semicircular, up to 12cm wide, dissected into flat, narrow segments. Flowers with 5 greenish-yellow sepals and 5 obovate petals, 6 to 15mm long, bright yellow. Shallow waters of marshes, ponds and ditches.

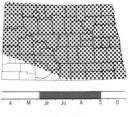

Bottineau County
August 1988

Black-eyed susan   *Rudbeckia hirta*

Stems erect, usually not branched, coursely hirsute, 3 to 6dm tall. Leaves alternate, those near base lanceolate and petioled, up to 15cm long; upper leaves sessile. Flowers solitary and terminal on stems, orangish-yellow with a brown, dome-shaped disk; with 8 to 21 ligules, each 2 to 4cm long; occasional flowers with reddish-brown spots at base. Common on prairies and in ditches, especially where moist.

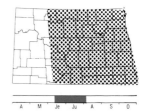

(Left) Grand Forks County
July 1967
(Right) McHenry County
June 1987

Leafy spurge   *Euphorbia esula*

Stems erect, clustered, often branched above, smooth, 3 to 9dm tall. Leaves oblanceolate with rounded apex, 1-nerved, 3 to 10cm long and 3 to 10mm wide; leaves of inflorescence more rounded. Inflorescence an umbel at the ends of branches. Flowers unisexual and greatly reduced; borne in a cup-shaped structure (cyathium) with 4 or 5 lobes, each cyathium with 1 female and numerous male flowers. An introduced weed that is common in ditches, pastures, and prairies.

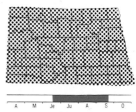

Grand Forks County
July 1964

Buffalo bur   *Solanum rostratum*

Stems erect, branched, with yellow spines, pubescent, 3 to 7dm tall. Leaves alternate, obovate, pinnately lobed, lobes rounded, 1 to 2dm long and 3 to 7cm wide. Inflorescence a raceme, the axis elongating in fruit. Flowers bright yellow, 5 to 15 per cluster; petals 5, united into a funnel with the lobes triangular and flared. Fruit a berry enclosed in a spiny bur. Common in pastures, ditches, and road edges.

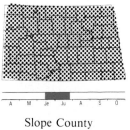

Slope County
June 1988

Fringed loosestrife   *Lysimachia ciliata*

Stems erect, usually unbranched, 3 to 10dm tall. Leaves opposite, petioled, ovate-lanceolate, 4 to 13cm long, ciliate (= fringed) on petioles and leaf apices, thereby giving rise to parts of both the common and scientific names. Flowers solitary in apical leaf axils, with long pedicels; with 5 yellow, pointed petals united at the base; 1 to 2cm wide. Locally common in moist woods and pond margins. The flowers are short-lived as the petals fall off readily.

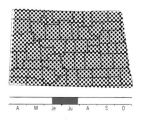

Bottineau County
June 1988

Prairie coneflower   *Ratibida columnifera*

Stems erect, very slender, singular or clustered, 3 to 10dm tall. Leaves alternate, pinnatifid, up to 15cm long and 6cm wide, densely pubescent. Flowering heads usually solitary; receptacle columnar; with 4 to 11 yellow ligules, 1 to 3cm long, usually reflexed. In the form *pulcherrima*, the ligules are reddish brown and yellow (see cover photograph). Very common in upland priaires and adjacent ditches. The common name comes from the columnar disk of the flower.

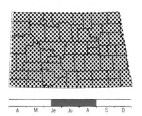

Grand Forks County
July 1964

58

Field sow thistle *Sonchus arvensis*

Stems erect, usually branched, reddish, 4 to 15dm tall, with a milky sap. Leaves alternate; lower ones pinnately lobed with short petioles, 6 to 40cm long and up to 15cm wide; upper leaves smaller, with fewer lobes and more nearly sessile; leaf margins prickly. Inflorescence a terminal corymbiform cluster of several heads 2.5 to 3.5cm wide, of ray florets only, golden yellow. Fruiting heads are white balls of plumose seeds. An introduced weed that is common in fields, pastures, roadsides, and other disturbed sites.

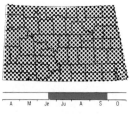

Grand Forks County
August 1962

Common sow thistle *Sonchus oleraceus*

This plant is similar to field sow thistle, but the flowering heads are pale yellow and less than 2.5cm wide. It is also an introduced weed and is found in similar habitats. A third species, prickly sow thistle (*Sonchus asper*), is very similar to common sow thistle but has rounded (instead of acute) leaf auricles.

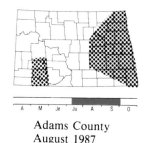

Adams County
August 1987

Bird's-foot trefoil *Lotus corniculatus*

Stems multiple from base, erect or decumbent, up to 6dm tall but usually much less. Leaves alternate, pinnately compound with 5 leaflets, the lower 2 reduced to stipules; leaflets obovate to broadly lanceolate. Inflorescence a 3- to 8-flowered umbel from leaf axils. Flowers yellow to orange-red; banner 12 to 16mm long, ovate or roundish; wings 10 to 14mm long, oblong; keel 12 to 14mm long, incurved. Introduced, now naturalized. Frequently planted in ditches where it is now often abundant. The common name comes from the slender pods, which resemble birds' feet.

Cass County
July 1988

61

Golden aster   *Chrysopsis villosa*

Stems erect, branched, rough hairy, 3 to 5dm tall. Leaves alternate, grayish-green due to pubescence, oblanceolate, petiolate below, becoming sessile above, 1 to 3cm long and 3 to 8mm wide. Flowers in clusters of 3 to 30 heads at ends of branches; with both ray and disk florets; golden yellow; with 15 to 30 ligules, each 8 to 12mm long. Common on upland prairies, badlands, sandhills, ditches, and road edges.

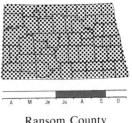

Ransom County
August 1987

Roundleaf monkey-flower   *Mimulus glabratus* var. *fremontii*

Stems prostrate, up to 4dm long. Leaves opposite, orbicular to reniform, 1 to 3cm long and 1.5 to 3cm wide, the upper ones sessile and the lower ones usually petiolate. Flowers with long pedicels, borne in the axils of leaves; petals yellow, bilabiate, the lower lip bearded. Uncommon in shallow water of streams or on adjacent banks. The generic name, *Mimulus*, and the common name, monkey-flower, both come from the appearance of a monkey's face on the flowers. A blue-flowered species is presented on p. 108.

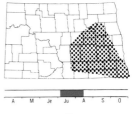

Barnes County
July 1988

Common evening primrose   *Oenothera villosa*

Stems erect, often branched, hirsute, 6 to 15dm tall. Leaves alternate, lanceolate, sessile or short-petioled, hirsute, 7 to 15cm long and 1 to 4cm wide. Flowers axillary, in terminal spikes; with a distinct floral tube; petals 4, obovate, yellow, 8 to 15mm long. Fruit a cylindric capsule tapering slightly toward the apex, 2 to 4.5cm long. Common in old fields and ditches and on roadsides. True to the common name, its flowers open in the evening. A very similar species is *Oenothera biennis*.

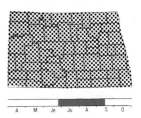

Bowman County
August 1987

Maximilian sunflower   *Helianthus maximilianii*

Stems erect, usually solitary, gray-green, 5 to 25dm tall; stems often clustered. Leaves mostly alternate, lanceolate, with short petioles, folded along the midrib and trough-shaped. Flowering heads few to many at ends of stems, 5 to 8cm wide, with both ray and disk florets, yellow, with 10 to 25 ray ligules. Very common in upland prairies, ditches, and similar sites. Six other kinds of sunflowers occur in North Dakota. The generic name literally means "sun flower."

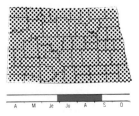

Grand Forks County
August 1962

Late goldenrod   *Solidago gigantea*

Stems erect, stout, smooth, 10 to 15dm tall; often clustered. Leaves mainly on stem, narrowly elliptic to lanceolate, 3-nerved, sessile or weakly petiolate, 6 to 17cm long and 1 to 4.5cm wide. Inflorescence a panicle with recurved-secund branches; terminal. Flowering heads with 10 to 18 ray florets and 6 to 10 disk florets; golden yellow. Abundant in local patches, especially around fens and in lowland prairies. There are 8 other species of yellow-flowered goldenrods in North Dakota, including the one below.

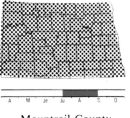

Mountrail County
August 1988

Rigid goldenrod   *Solidago rigida*

Stems erect, stout, rough, pubescent, 2 to 16dm tall; usually clustered. Basal leaves lanceolate to broadly ovate with a long petiole, 1 to 3dm long and 2 to 10cm wide; stem leaves alternate, progressively reduced and becoming sessile. Inflorescence terminal and corymbiform. Flowering heads consisting of 7 to 14 ray florets and 19 to 31 disk florets; golden yellow. Common in upland prairies, pastures and ditches.

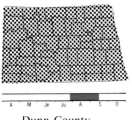

Dunn County
August 1988

64

Curly-top gumweed   *Grindelia squarrosa*

Stems erect, one to several, widely branched, 1 to 10dm tall. Leaves sessile, ovate to oblanceolate, finely toothed, thick, stiff, 1.5 to 7cm long and 4 to 20mm wide. Flowering heads terminal on branches, with sticky (gummy) base, with both ray and disk florets, yellow; with 12 to 37 ligules, each 7 to 15mm long. Common on upland prairies, saline lowland prairies, pastures, ditches, and road edges. American Indians used gumweed plants for a variety of medicinal purposes.

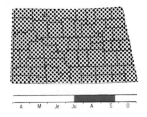

Grand Forks County
August 1959

Hawkweed   *Hieracium umbellatum*

Stem erect, 4 to 8dm tall, base glabrous, lightly pubescent above. Leaves alternate, numerous, ovate to lanceolate, sessile, irregularly dentate, up to 10 cm long and 2cm wide. Inflorescence a loose, corymbiform cluster with 40 or more heads. Flowering heads entirely ligulate, golden yellow, 1.5 to 2.5cm wide. Locally common in open woods, woods edges, prairies and ditches. The generic name is from the Greek word for hawk, hence the common name.

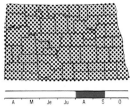

Bottineau County
August 1988

Spotted touch-me-not   *Impatiens capensis*

Stems erect, hollow, branched, 5 to 15dm tall; nodes somewhat swollen. Leaves alternate, ovate to elliptic, serrate, 3 to 10cm long. Flowers 1 to 3 in leaf axils, hanging on the peduncle; orangish-yellow with reddish spots; the large "petal" is a sepal with a 6 to 9mm long spur. Locally common in wet sites in woods and woods edges and on lake and stream margins. A related species, jewel weed (*Impatiens pallida*), has pale yellow flowers with few spots; it occurs in similar habitats but is much less common.

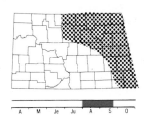

Ransom County
August 1982

Butter and eggs   *Linaria vulgaris*

Stems erect, sometimes branched, clustered, 3 to 6dm tall. Leaves usually alternate, sessile, linear, tapering to a subpetiolar base, 2.5 to 4cm long and 2 to 6mm wide. Inflorescence a raceme. Flowers with a ventral spur at base; bilabiate with a 2-lobed upper lip and a 3-lobed lower lip; bright yellow; throat with an orange-hairy palate; 1.8 to 2.8cm long. An introduced species locally common in ditches and roadsides; now naturalized. It gets its common name from the colors in its flowers.

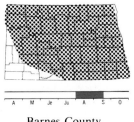

Barnes County
August 1987

Rabbit brush   *Chrysothamnus nauseosus graveolens*

Shrub with erect, branched stems covered with a grayish tomentum of long, entangled hairs, 2 to 15dm high. Leaves alternate, sessile, linear to linear-lanceolate, grayish-green, 2 to 6cm long and 1 to 2mm wide. Flowering heads numerous in terminal clusters; with 5 disk florets per head, no ray florets; yellow. A characteristic plant of badlands and dry, hilly upland prairies.

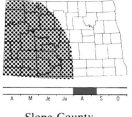

Slope County
August 1987

Snakeweed   *Gutierrezia sarothrae*

Stems erect, widely branched from a woody base, 2 to 10dm tall. Leaves alternate, linear, 5 to 60mm long and 1 to 3mm wide. Flowering heads numerous in terminal clusters, each head with 3 to 8 ray and 2 to 6 disk florets, golden yellow. Widespread and common on upland prairies, hillsides, and badlands.

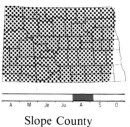

Slope County
August 1987

69

Beggar-ticks   *Bidens frondosa*

Stems erect, branched, sometimes purplish, pubescent, 2 to 10dm tall. Leaves opposite, pinnatifid with 3 to 5 lanceolate segments, petiolate, 5 to 15cm long. Flowering heads numerous at the ends of branches, with both ray and disk florets, golden yellow. The seeds (achenes) are flat, 2-awned, and barbed; they are well adapted to catch on fur and clothing, aiding dispersal. Common on stream banks, lake shores, ephemeral marshes, and wet spots in ditches. Four other species of beggar-ticks occur in similar habitats in North Dakota.

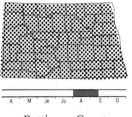

Bottineau County
August 1988

Sneezeweed   *Helenium autumnale*

Stems erect, solitary or branched, 3 to 10dm tall. Leaves alternate, oblong to lanceolate, base subsessile and decurrent, 4 to 15cm long and up to 4cm wide. Flowering heads several in an open cluster; flowers 2 to 3cm wide on long peduncles, with 10 or more 3-lobed ligules; both ligules and disk yellow, the disk dome-shaped. Locally common in open moist sites such as ditches adjacent to woods.

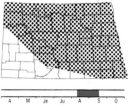

Ransom County
August 1987

Golden glow   *Rudbeckia laciniata*

Stems erect, branched, smooth, 0.5 to 2m tall. Leaves alternate, deeply pinnatifid or trilobed, toothed, 1 to 2dm long. Flowering heads one to several at ends of branches; with 8 to 13 yellow ligules, each 3 to 6cm long; disk somewhat hemispheric. Common in open moist woods and open moist sites adjacent to woods.

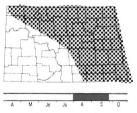

Ransom County
August 1982

70

71

Red

Columbine   *Aquilegia canadensis*

Stem erect, stout, branched, villous or smooth, 3 to 8dm tall. Leaves alternate, compound, with 3 leaflets that are often secondarily lobed; upper leaves reduced in size. Flowers nodding; formed of 5 reddish sepals alternating with 5 reddish petals; petals with yellowish upper parts and prolonged into narrow, bulbous-tipped spurs. Common in open woods and woods edges.

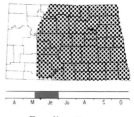

Cavalier County
May 1987

Red false mallow   *Sphaeralcea coccinea*

Stem single or clustered, usually decumbent, up to 20cm tall. Leaves alternate, petiolate, compound with 3 to 5 oblong to oblanceolate segments, densely gray pubescent. Inflorescence a raceme at the ends of short branches. Flowers with 5 sepals and 5 petals; petals 1 to 2cm long, orange to brick red; centers bright yellow because of the numerous stamens. Locally abundant in dry, gravelly soils on prairies, badlands, and roadsides.

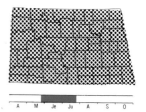

Golden Valley County
June 1984

Wild lily   *Lilium philadelphicum*

Stem erect, solitary, 3 to 9dm tall, arising from a bulb deep in the soil. Leaves numerous, alternate on stem, but whorled below flower; linear, 4 to 7.5cm long and 3 to 10mm wide. Flowers 1 to 3 in a terminal cluster, with 3 sepals and 3 petals, all orange-red to deep red with yellow centers and dark spots. In wet prairies and moist parts of rich upland prairies; often abundant where protected from grazing and haying until late in the season.

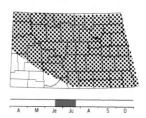

Grand Forks County
July 1965

Pink

Torch flower   *Geum triflorum*

Stems erect, pubescent, 2 to 4dm tall, clumped. Leaves mostly basal, petioled, 5 to 15cm long, pinnately compound, with 7 to 19 irregularly-lobed leaflets increasing in size from base to apex. Inflorescence cymose. Flowers usually 3 to a stem, hence the species name, *triflorum*; nodding, purplish. Fruiting heads erect and plumose, giving rise to another common name, "prairie smoke." Occasionally common in upland prairie and ditches.

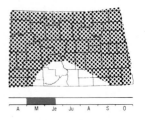

Stutsman County
June 1982
(Fruit) McLean County
June 1988

American vetch   *Vicia americana*

Stem vining, erect, or spreading, 2 to 10dm long. Leaves pinnately compound with 4 to 14 opposite leaflets; terminal leaflet modified into a tendril with which the leaf attaches to an object. Inflorescence an axillary, spikelike raceme of 3 to 10 flowers. Flowers 12 to 25mm long, pink to bluish-purple; banner longer than the wings and keel. Frequent in open woodlands, less common in prairies. A second species, the hairy vetch (*Vicia villosa*), also occurs in the state but is rare.

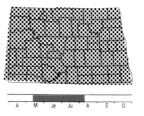

Pembina County
June 1988

Two-grooved vetch   *Astragalus bisulcatus*

Stem erect or decumbent, branched, forming clumps, 2 to 7dm tall. Leaves alternate, pinnately compound with 15 to 35 leaflets. Inflorescence an axillary raceme on a 3 to 12cm long peduncle; racemes many-flowered, flowers reflexed. Petals purple, occasionally whitish; banner 10 to 17mm long; keel 6 to 13mm long, rounded. Fruit pendulous with two prominent grooves on the upper surface. Common in ditches, pastures and prairies, especially in western counties.

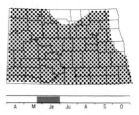

Slope County
June 1988

74

Scarlet gaura *Gaura coccinea*

Stems several, erect, branched, 2 to 5dm tall. Leaves linear, 0.5 to 4 cm long and 1 to 7mm wide, decreasing in size upwards. Inflorescence a terminal, spicate raceme, 5 to 40cm long. Flowers sessile, each with a small, basal bract; with 4 petals, 3 to 7mm long, white on opening in late afternoon, becoming pink to reddish-brown when fading the next day. Common on upland prairies and along roadsides.

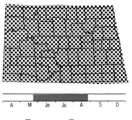

Sargent County
August 1987

Spreading dogbane *Apocynum androsaemifolium*

Stems erect, stiff, branched, 1 to 6dm tall; with a milky sap. Leaves opposite, short-petiolate, broadly ovate to elliptic, horizontal or drooping. Inflorescence a terminal or axillary corymbose cyme. Flowers campanulate, 6 to 9mm long, pinkish with deep pink veins inside. Common along the edges of woods, occasional in prairies and ditches. A second species, Indian hemp dogbane (*Apocynum cannabinum*), also occurs in the state; it has smaller, white flowers and erect or ascending leaves.

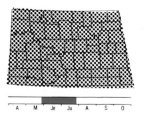

Pembina County
June 1988

Pincushion cactus *Coryphantha vivipara*

Stems solitary or clumped, globose, up to 10 to 12cm in diameter and 7 to 9cm tall; with spirally-arranged tubercles that have areoles on apical surfaces; areoles with sharp spines, one to several of which extend straight out, the others extending laterally. Flowers large (to 4cm across) and pink to reddish-purple. Prairies, badlands and sandy ditches. A related species, *Coryphantha missouriensis*), is similar in appearance but has yellow flowers.

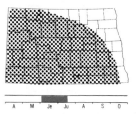

Burleigh County
June 1982

76

Prairie wild rose   *Rosa arkansana*

Stems erect, branched, somewhat woody, sparsely to densely covered with unequal prickles; partially or completely dying back to the ground each year. Leaves alternate, petiolate; pinnately compound with 9 to 11 leaflets, 1 to 4cm long, serrate. Inflorescence corymbose on ends of new growth or lateral branches of old stems. Flowers with 5 deep rose petals which fade to pale pink. North Dakota's state flower. Common on prairies and in ditches; also occurs in open woods.

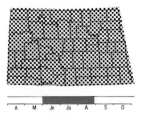

Grand Forks County
July 1962

Prickly wild rose   *Rosa acicularis*

Stem course, bristly, densely branched, woody, to 1.2m in height. Leaves alternate, petiolate; pinnately compound with 5 to 7 leaflets, 1.5 to 5cm long. Flowers similar to those of the prairie wild rose. Occasional at the edges of woods and on wooded hillsides. A similar species is the smooth wild rose (*Rosa blanda*), which has the upper branches free of bristles; it also occurs in or near woods.

Cavalier County
June 1988

Hairy four-o-clock   *Mirabilis hirsuta*

Stems erect, 2 to 8dm tall, densely hirsute; Leaves opposite, variable in shape, usually ovate to oblong, hirsute. Inflorescence terminal, axillary cymes. Flowers 8 to 10mm long, with 5 deep pink, petal-like sepals joined to form a tubular flower of 5 lobes; no petals. Occurs in upland prairies and ditches, especially on dry, sandy soils. The name, four-o-clock, comes from the habit of the flowers opening in late afternoon. The hirsute stems and leaves give the species its name, *hirsuta*. Three other species of four-o-clocks occur in the state.

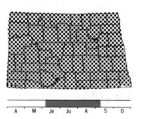

Foster County
August 1987

78

Musk thistle   *Carduus nutans* var. *leiophyllus*

Biennial; stemless in first year; with a 0.5 to 3m tall, spiny, much branched stem bearing flowers in the second year. Leaves forming a basal rosette on the ground the first year; stem leaves of second-year plant alternate, lobed, and very spiny. Flowering heads nodding, usually becoming fully erect in full bloom; 5 to 7cm in diameter; deep pink. This is a showy, but noxious introduced weed that is locally common in pastures.

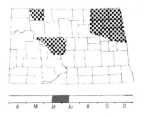

A   M   Je   Ju   A   S   O

Grand Forks County
June 1987

Wolfberry   *Symphoricarpos occidentalis*

Shrub 0.5 to 1m tall, forming large, brushy colonies. Leaves opposite, petiolate, usually ovate or elliptic, 2 to 6cm long and 1 to 3.5cm wide, whitish pubescent on the undersurface. Inflorescence terminal and axillary spikes, containing 2 to 12 pale pink, campanulate flowers, each about 5 to 8mm long. Fruit globose and whitish, becoming black with age. This very common shrub occurs in woods, on prairies and pastures, and in ditches.

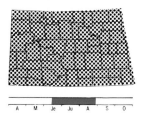

A   M   Je   Ju   A   S   O

Griggs County
July 1982

Skeletonweed   *Lygodesmia juncea*

Stems erect, many-branched, smooth, green, usually less than 4dm tall, with a yellow milky juice; often with globose galls produced by insects. Leaves few; basal ones linear; stem leaves reduced to tiny scales. Flowers in solitary heads at ends of branches, usually with 5 ray florets but no disk florets; ligules lavender, 10 to 12mm long. Common on prairies and in ditches, especially where soils are sandy. The common name of this plant comes from the near absence of leaves.

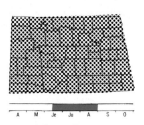

A   M   Je   Ju   A   S   O

Adams County
August 1987

80

81

Showy milkweed   *Asclepias speciosa*

Stems erect, usually solitary and stout, minutely pubescent, 5 to 10dm tall, with milky sap. Leaves opposite, short-petioled, broadly lanceolate to ovate, 8 to 20cm long and 2.5 to 10cm wide, densely pubescent underneath. Inflorescence an axillary cyme with up to 40 rose-colored flowers, 15 to 28mm tall; with 5 petals modified into large, spreading hoods, 9 to 15mm long, each with a prominent horn. Fruit a 7 to 11cm long pod with plumose seeds. Frequent in moist prairies, open draws, and ditches. Common milkweed (*Asclepias syriaca*), with more numerous, smaller flowers, is similar.

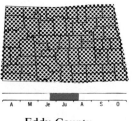

Eddy County
June 1988

Swamp milkweed   *Asclepias incarnata*

Stems solitary, stout, much branched above, 1 to 2m tall, with a milky sap, hence the name "milkweed." Leaves opposite, lanceolate, short-petioled, 5 to 15cm long and 1 to 3cm wide. Inflorescence a cyme with 10 to 40 flowers at ends of stems and branches. Flowers pale to deep pink, 9 to 11mm tall; with 5 petals modified into short erect hoods, each with a small horn. Seeds plumose and contained within a 5 to 8cm long pod. Locally common along edges of ponds, lakes, and rivers.

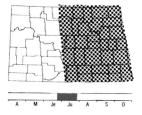

Nelson County
June 1988

Purple coneflower   *Echinacea angustifolia*

Stems erect, sometimes branched, hirsute, 1 to 6dm tall. Leaves alternate, lanceolate to oblong, up to 30cm long and 4cm wide; lower ones petiolate, upper ones sessile. Flowers solitary on long peduncles; heads 5 to 8cm across; ligules pale pink to purplish, 2 to 4cm long, spreading; disk brown, dome-shaped, prickly. Common on upland prairies and badlands, also on the drier slopes of ditches. The generic name comes from the Greek word for hedgehog, supposedly because the disk resembles a hedgehog.

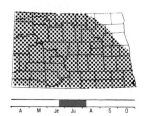

Golden Valley County
June 1988

Swamp smartweed *Polygonum amphibium* var. *emersum*

Stems erect, with slightly swollen nodes, often reaching 1m in height. Leaves alternate, short petiolate, ovate to lanceolate, often with undulate margins, up to 25cm long and 6cm wide; with stipules forming a sheath around the stem. Inflorescence erect, spiciform racemes, 2 to 15cm long, solitary or paired at the end of branches. Flowers pink. Common in marshes, shallow water ditches, and wet meadows. Fourteen other species of smartweed occur in the state.

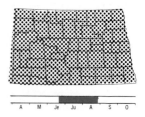

Grand Forks County
July 1962

Rocky Mountain bee plant *Cleome serrulata*

Stems erect, branched, 2 to 15dm tall. Leaves alternate, petiolate; palmately compound, with 3 lanceolate leaflets, 2 to 6cm long and 5 to 15mm wide. Inflorescence a terminal, many-flowered raceme. Flowers on 14 to 20cm long pedicels, with 4 pink petals; with 6 stamens, 1 to 2cm long, much longer than the petals. Fruit an elongate capsule pointed at both ends, drooping. Frequent in upland prairies and roadsides. This is closely related to a cultivated plant, the spider flower.

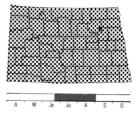

Slope County
August 1988

Wild bergamot *Monarda fistulosa*

Stems erect, simple or branched above, square, 3 to 12dm tall. Leaves usually lanceolate with a serrate margin, petiolate, and 3 to 10cm long. When crushed, the leaves have a characteristic minty odor. Flower heads solitary, terminal, 5 to 10cm wide. Flowers with petals partially united, 2 to 3.5cm long, tubular with upper and lower lips, pale to deep pink. Locally common, often in extensive colonies, in prairies and wooded draws. Beebalm, a cultivated plant, is a related species.

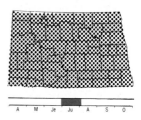

McKenzie County
July 1973

84

Purple prairie clover   *Dalea purpurea*

Stem usually erect, pubescent, 3 to 9dm tall. Leaves alternate, pinnately compound, usually with 5 linear leaflets, 10 to 24mm long; with a fragrant odor when crushed. Inflorescence a dense, conelike, terminal spike 1 to 7cm long. Flowers with pink to deep rose petals. Purple prairie clover is common on upland prairies and pastures, also some ditches. It is closely related to the species below and to white prairie clover, *Dalea candida*, which is illustrated in the frontispiece.

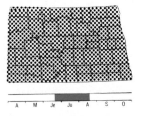

Grand Forks County
August 1965

Silky prairie clover   *Dalea villosa*

Stems erect or spreading, usually branched, densely villose, 2 to 3.5dm tall, giving a bushy appearance. Leaves alternate, pinnately compound, with from 11 to 21 leaflets, 2 to 4cm long, densely villose, grayish. Inflorescence a terminal spike, 3 to 12cm long, somewhat drooping. Flowers with deep pink petals. Characteristic of sand dunes and sandy prairies.

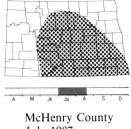

McHenry County
July 1987

American germander   *Teucrium canadense*

Stems erect, simple or sparingly branched, square, 3 to 10dm tall. Leaves opposite, petiolate, ovate to lanceolate with serrate margins, 3 to 12cm long and 1 to 4cm wide. Inflorescence a terminal spike. Flowers with light to deep pink petals united into a tube with upper and lower lips; upper lip with 2 narrow, diverging lobes, lower lip broad with several dark pink streaks. Common on river banks and lake shores.

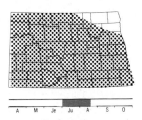

Barnes County
July 1988

86

Canada tickclover   *Desmodium canadense*

Stems erect, branched, pilose, 0.5 to 1m tall. Leaves alternate, petiolate, and pinnately compound with 3 ovate leaflets. Inflorescence a densely flowered, terminal raceme. Flowers 8 to 13mm long, deep pink, becoming bluish on fading. Fruit an elongate, compressed pod containing 3 to 5 seeds. The seed segments are known as "sticktights" because they attach readily to hairs and clothing by means of their hooked hairs. Occurs usually in grassy areas adjacent to woods.

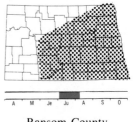

Ransom County
July 1988

Fireweed   *Epilobium angustifolium circumvagum*

Stems erect, stout, solitary or branched, from 3 to 25dm high. Leaves spirally arranged and lanceolate, 2.5 to 20cm long and 0.4 to 3.5cm wide. Inflorescence an elongate terminal raceme. Flowers with 4 deep pink petals, 8 stamens and a conspicuous 4-lobed stigma. Fruit an elongate, slender pod containing many seeds. Usually found in patches on disturbed sites where the showy flowers are conspicuous. The name "fireweed" comes from the frequent occurrence of this plant on burned land.

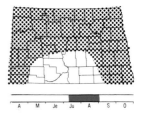

Rolette County
August 1987

Gay-feather   *Liatris pycnostachya*

Stems erect, stiff, unbranched, and 5 to 15dm tall. Leaves alternate, linear, up to 4dm long, and much reduced in length on upper parts of stem. Inflorescence an elongate spike of numerous sessile heads; heads small, with 5 to 7 disk florets each, pink to rose in color; no ray florets. Flowers bloom from the top of the inflorescence down. Occurs in moist lowland prairie and ditches. Three other species of *Liatris* occur on prairies in North Dakota.

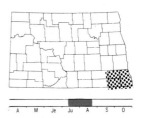

Richland County
July 1988

Pink wild onion   *Allium stellatum*

Plants without a stem; leaves and flower arising from an underground bulb. Leaves linear, 1 to 4mm wide, arising at ground level, usually withering during flowering. Inflorescence an umbel at top of a scape, taller than leaves. Flowers deep pink, the 3 sepals and 3 petals similar, star-shaped (hence the species name, *stellatum*). Common in prairies and wet meadows. There are 2 other wild onions, white wild onion, which is common across the state, and wild leek, which occurs in eastern woods.

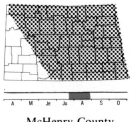

McHenry County
July 1987

Obedient plant   *Physostegia parviflora*

Stems square, erect, branching, 2 to 15dm tall. Leaves lanceolate, sessile and clasping, 4 to 12cm long, 7 to 20mm wide, margins usually serrate. Inflorescences terminal on branches, spike-like, 1 to 2dm long. Flowers rose-purple, tubular, with upper and lower lips, 9 to 12mm long. Locally abundant along stream banks. The flowers are unusual; if pushed to one side, they remain in the new position, hence the common name "obedient plant."

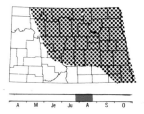

Stutsman County
August 1982

Gerardia   *Agalinis aspera*

Stems erect, slender, with ascending branches, 2 to 6dm tall. Leaves opposite, sessile, linear, sharp-tipped, usually revolute, 2 to 4cm long and 1 to 1.5mm wide. Flowers solitary at upper leaf bases, pink to rose purple, with spreading lobes, 18 to 25mm long and 1 to 1.5cm wide. Uncommon in wet meadows. Gerardia is unusual in that the leaves and stems blacken upon drying.

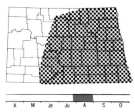

McHenry County
August 1988

91

Common burdock   *Arctium minus*

Biennial. Stems erect, branched, 0.5 to 2dm tall. Basal leaves ovate, cordate, 3 to 6dm long and 3 to 4dm wide, green above and whitish below, with stout hollow petioles 1 to 4dm long; upper leaves similar but much smaller. Flowers in subglobose heads clustered at ends of branches; pink to purplish; sharp spiny bracts at base of flower. Introduced weed common in woods and pastures. The dried flowers are burs that stick to fur and clothing. The leaves and petioles resemble rhubarb; petioles are not edible.

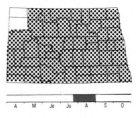

Barnes County
August 1987

Joe-pye weed   *Eupatorium maculatum* var. *bruneri*

Stems erect, purplish, 4 to 10dm tall. Leaves in whorls of 4s and 5s, lanceolate, with serrate margins, 6 to 15cm long and 2 to 8cm wide. Inflorescence a modified cyme, flat-topped. Flower heads with 9 to 22 disk florets, purple; without ray florets. Locally common in marshy areas.

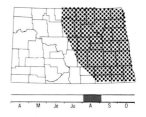

Ransom County
August 1982

Hog peanut   *Amphicarpaea bracteata*

Slender twining vine, 3 to 20dm long. Leaves alternate, trifoliate; leaflets lanceolate to ovate, 2 to 10cm long and 1.8 to 7cm wide. Flowers in axillary racemes, pale lilac, 10 to 15mm long. Occurring in woods and woods edges. Hog peanuts have 2 types of flowers; the second type develops at ground level, grows into the ground and forms the ''peanut,'' which is edible.

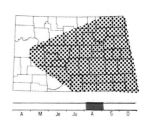

Ransom County
August 1982

93

Blue-Purple

Pasque flower   *Anemone patens*

Stems erect, densely villous, 1 to 3dm tall. Leaves with 3 to 7-lobed blades that are deeply subdivided; basal leaves petiolate, densely villous; basal leaves often not developing until end of flowering. Flowers solitary on ends of tall stalks, 4 to 8cm across; with 5 to 8 oval sepals, 1.8 to 4cm long, pale lavender to bluish; no petals. Fruiting head subglobose, seeds with long plumes. Locally abundant on undisturbed upland prairies. This is the earliest prairie flower.

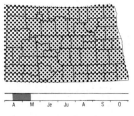

Sheridan County
April 1988

Blue prairie violet   *Viola pratincola*

Plant erect, without an obvious stem. Leaves arising from the ground, glabrous, cordate to ovate; margin with fine teeth or lobes. Flowers solitary on long peduncles; petals pale to deep purple, whitish at center and usually with darker violet veins, especially on lower 3 petals; lateral 2 petals bearded; 12 to 18mm long. Common in open woodlands, occasional in moist prairies. Four other species of purple-flowered violets occur in the state.

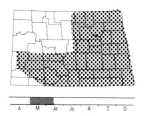

Grand Forks County
May 1988

Blue-eyed grass   *Sisyrinchium montanum*

Plant grass-like. Stem erect, flattened, winged, up to 3dm tall, 2mm wide. Leaves linear, erect, about 2mm wide, shorter than the stem. Flowers several in a terminal cluster, emerging from a spathe; only one or two opening at a time; with 3 sepals and 3 petals, each with a pointed tip; pale blue to violet with yellow center. Common in native prairies and wet meadows, occasional in open, grassy woods. Another species, *Sisyrinchium mucronatum*, has been recorded from eastern North Dakota.

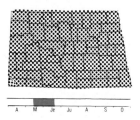

Barnes County
May 1988

Bluebells   *Mertensia lanceolata*

Stem erect, glabrous, 3 to 4dm tall. Leaves
alternate; basal leaves petiolate, ovate to
lanceolate, up to 14cm long and 4cm wide;
stem leaves sessile, lanceolate. Inflorescence a cyme from axils of upper
leaves, flowers drooping. Corolla of united
petals, tubular, 5-lobed, 10 to 15mm long;
pink in bud, becoming blue. Calyx of 5
green sepals, about half as long as petals,
pointed. Occurs on upland prairies and
badlands. *Mertensia oblongifolia* also occurs in the state.

Slope County
June 1982

Blue flax   *Linum perenne* var. *lewisii*

Stems erect, basally-branched, slender,
leafy, 5 to 8dm tall. Leaves linear to linear-
lanceolate, 1 to 3cm long and 1 to 2mm
wide. Inflorescence a few-branched panicle. Flowers pedicellate, showy, with 5 pale
blue petals 10 to 15mm long. Common on
upland prairies and roadsides. A related
species, common flax (*Linum usitatissi-
mum*), is cultivated in fields and may grow
along roadsides where seeds have fallen
from grain trucks.

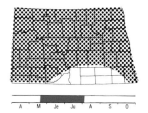

Golden Valley County
June 1983

Brooklime speedwell   *Veronica americana*

Aquatic plant with erect, spreading stems
1 to 6cm long. Leaves opposite, petiolate,
lanceolate to ovate, usually glabrous; 1 to
3cm long and 1 to 2cm wide. Inflorescence
an axillary raceme, 10 to 25-flowered.
Flowers pedicellate; corolla short-tubular,
irregularly 4-lobed; petals blue, 5 to 10mm
long and wide. Occurs along edges of rivers
and brooks, rarely other wet sites. Six additional species of speedwells occur in the
state.

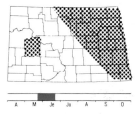

Barnes County
May 1988

Missouri milk-vetch   *Astragalus missouriensis*

Stems prostrate or tufted, silvery-white, hairy, 1 to 4cm long. Leaves alternate, hairy, grayish, pinnately compound with 9 to 17 leaflets, each 7 to 13mm long. Inflorescence an axillary raceme, 5 to 15-flowered; flowering stalk 10 to 15cm tall, hairy, grayish. Flowers rose-purple; banner 14 to 24mm long; keel 12 to 18mm long, rounded. This showy flower is frequently found in upland prairie and ditches, especially in the western part of the state.

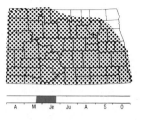

Dunn County
June 1988

Purple locoweed   *Oxytropis lambertii*

Plant forming a small clump of leaves and flowering stalks, usually 4 to 5cm tall. Leaves few, arising from the ground; pinnately compound with 7 to 19 leaflets, pubescent. Inflorescence a 10 to 20-flowered raceme on a 5 to 30cm tall peduncle. Flowers deep pink to purple; banner 15 to 25mm long; keel 13 to 19mm long, pointed. Fruit a long, slender pod with a sharp tip. Common in prairie and ditches. The plant is poisonous to livestock.

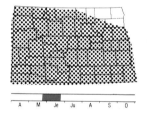

Logan County
June 1982

Spiderwort   *Tradescantia bracteata*

Stems erect, usually unbranched, 2 to 6dm tall, with 2 to 4 conspicuous nodes; internodes 10 to 20cm long. Leaves alternate, linear-lanceolate, 8 to 30cm long and 7 to 16mm wide. Inflorescence a solitary, terminal cyme, usually few-flowered. Flowers with 3 narrow, acute, pale-purplish sepals and 3 ovate, deep pink to purple petals. Frequent in wet meadows and moist, sandy ditches, especially in the eastern part of the state. A related species, *Tradescantia occidentalis*, is more common in western North Dakota.

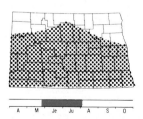

Ransom County
August 1987

Crested beardtongue   *Penstemon eriantherus*

Stems, erect, slender, solitary or several in group, villose, grayish-green, 2 to 4dm tall. Leaves opposite, clasping, lanceolate to oblong, sometimes serrate; pubescent. Inflorescence a terminal, compound panicle. Flowers with petals united, funnel-shaped, bilabiate, abruptly inflated, lavender; upper lip 2-lobed, lower lip 3-lobed; with a false stamen bearing numerous golden hairs in throat opening; 22 to 35cm long. Occurs in upland prairies and badlands.

McKenzie County
June 1988

Slender beardtongue   *Penstemon gracilis*

Stems erect, slender, solitary or several, 2 to 5dm tall, greenish, but often reddish in upper portions. Leaves opposite, clasping, linear to lanceolate, with serrate margins, 2.5 to 8cm long and 4 to 15mm wide. Inflorescence a terminal, compound panicle, 1 to 2dm long. Flowers with petals united, narrowly funnel-shaped, pale lavender, bilabiate, 15 to 22mm long. Occurs in prairies and roadsides.

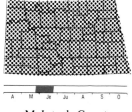

McIntosh County
June 1982

Harebell   *Campanula rotundifolia*

Stems erect, slender, often clumped, 1.5 to 7dm tall. Leaves of 2 kinds, the lowermost ovate and the upper ones linear to oblanceolate, sessile. Flowers solitary or in terminal or axillary clusters; petals united into a 5-lobed, campanulate, blue flower, 10 to 20mm long. Our only native bellflower, it is common on prairies and in ditches, especially on moist soil; occasional in open woods. An introduced species, creeping bellflower (*Campanula rapunculoides*), occurs along roads and in disturbed sites.

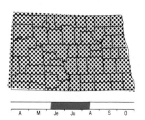

Grand Forks County
June 1988

100

101

Marsh skullcap   *Scutellaria galericulata*

Stems erect, delicate, square, single or branched, 2 to 6dm tall. Leaves opposite, thin, lanceolate-ovate, shallowly serrate, 3 to 6cm long and 1 to 2cm wide, reduced in size upwards. Flowers 2 per node in upper leaf axils; blue; about 2cm long. Usually found along stream banks and lake shores, occasionally in adjacent moist woods. The word "skullcap" refers to the ascending, shieldlike protrusion, the scutellum, on the upper lobe of the calyx.

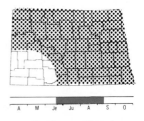

Bottineau County
June 1988

Lavender hyssop   *Agastache foeniculum*

Stems square, erect, solitary or slightly branched, from 6 to 12dm tall. Leaves broadly ovate, 4 to 9cm long, densely pubescent on undersides. Inflorescence a terminal spike, sometimes with clusters in upper leaf axils. Flowers bilabiate with each petal formed into an upper lip that is 2-lobed and a lower lip that is 3-lobed; petals bluish-purple; stamens and style prominently exserted. Common in moist woods and along wooded lakeshores. Plants have an anise-like odor.

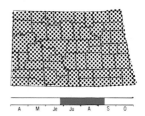

Bottineau County
June 1988

Lead plant   *Amorpha canescens*

Shrub. Stems erect, branched, becoming woody at base, pubescent, 3 to 8dm tall. Leaves alternate, pinnately compound with 27 to 41 ovate to elliptic leaflets each. Inflorescence a dense raceme, 7 to 15cm long, in the axils of upper leaves. Flowers with one violet petal and bright orange stamens. Frequent in upland prairies, roadsides, and open woodlands. The common name comes from the grayish coloration of the plant. The leaves were used by Indians to make a tea and for medicinal purposes.

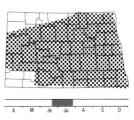

Eddy County
June 1988

Small lupine   *Lupinus pusillus*

Stems erect, single or branched, hirsute, 0.5 to 2dm tall. Leaves alternate, petiolate, palmately compound with 6 to 8 oblanceolate leaflets. Inflorescence a terminal raceme. Flowers 1cm long, of leguminous type; color ranging from white to purple, usually pale blue with a whitish keel. Frequent on upland prairies and badlands, especially on sandy soils. Another lupine, silvery lupine (*Lupinus argenteus*), has similar distribution in the state.

Slope County
June 1984

Silver-leaf scurf-pea   *Psoralea argophylla*

Stems erect, branched, 4 to 5dm tall. Leaves alternate, petiolate, palmately compound, usually with 3 to 5 obovate leaflets. Stems and leaves are conspicuously pubescent, giving the plant a grayish appearance. Inflorescence a terminal or axillary raceme of 2 to 5 whorls of 3 to 6 flowers each, on long peduncles. Flowers bluish-purple, small, barely exceeding the grayish calyx lobes. Common on upland prairies and roadside ditches. *Psoralea esculenta*, the prairie-turnip, has an edible root.

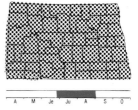

McKenzie County
July 1973

Blue lettuce   *Lactuca oblongifolia*

Stems erect, solitary or clustered, up to 1m tall, with a milky sap. Leaves linear to oblong, entire or pinnately lobed, 9 to 13cm long and 1 to 3cm wide. Inflorescence a panicle of 20 to 50 heads. Flowers 1.5 to 2cm across, of ray florets (19-21) only; ligule 9 to 10mm long, pale bluish-purple. Common, often in patches, on prairies and in roadside ditches, especially where the soil is fairly moist.

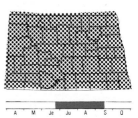

Grand Forks County
July 1967

Ironweed   *Vernonia fasciculata corymbosa*

Stem erect, often reddish, 3 to 6dm tall,
branched at top. Leaves alternate,
lanceolate with serrate edges, 3.5 to 10cm
long, pitted on the undersurface. Inflorescence a flat-topped cluster of heads,
each head with 10 to 26 disk florets; no ray
florets. Flowers purple. Occasional in
moist prairies and ditches. The name
"ironweed" comes from the tough structure of the stems.

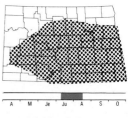

Richland County
July 1988

Wavy-leaf thistle   *Cirsium undulatum*

Stem erect, stout, usually solitary,
sometimes branched above, 4 to 10dm tall,
gray with dense pubescence. Some leaves
lanceolate and toothed, most pinnate with
undulate margins and lobes tipped with a
yellow spine; gray pubescent, especially on
undersurface. Flowering heads solitary and
terminal, 4 to 7cm wide, of disk florets only, purple. Common in patches on prairies,
pastures, and ditches. A related species,
Cirsium flodmanii, is similar, but seldom
forms patches and often begins flowering
about a month later.

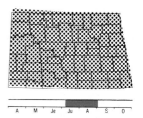

Richland County
July 1988

Bull thistle   *Cirsium vulgare*

Biennial; stem of second-year plant erect,
branched, spiny-winged, green. Leaves
lanceolate, deeply pinnately lobed and with
apical spines, green with fine yellowish
prickles on upper surface. Flowering heads
solitary at ends of branches; base of flower
with many sharp-pointed, recurved bracts;
flower of disk florets only, purple, 3 to 4cm
wide. Occasional in pastures, ditches, and
disturbed sites. Introduced.

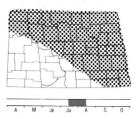

Sargent County
July 1988

107

Blue vervain   *Verbena hastata*

Stems erect, up to 2m tall, usually branched above, with rough pubescent surface. Leaves opposite, petiolate, lanceolate with serrate margins, up to 18cm long. Inflorescence a spoke of many flowers at the ends of branches; petals united to form a 5-lobed flower with a short, tubular base, purplish-blue, 3-4mm wide. Frequent along streams and lake shores; also sometimes found in wet meadows.

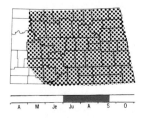

Ransom County
August 1982

Hoary vervain   *Verbena stricta*

Stem erect, up to 12dm tall, usually branched above, 4-angled, densely hairy. Leaves opposite, sessile, ovate with serrate margins, up to 7cm long. Inflorescence an erect spike up to 3dm long; one or several terminating each branch; petals united to form a 5-lobed flower with a short, tubular base, purple, 8-9mm wide. Common on prairies, pastures, ditches, and disturbed sites.

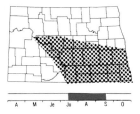

Richland County
August 1987

Alleghany monkey-flower   *Mimulus ringens*

Stems erect, often branched, conspicuously 4-angled, 2 to 13dm tall. Leaves opposite, sessile, clasping, oblanceolate, 2 to 8cm long and 6 to 20mm wide. Flowers solitary in the axils of upper leaves, with a long (20 to 45mm) pedicel; bilabiate, tubular, lavender; 2 to 3cm long. Infrequent in the edges of streams and ponds and on sandbars in rivers.

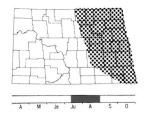

Stutsman County
August 1982

Purple loosestrife   *Lythrum salicaria*

Stems several, erect, up to 12dm high. Leaves opposite or whorled, lanceolate, up to 10cm long and 15mm wide. Flowers in terminal spikes, with 6 rose-purple petals each. Occasional in ditches and marshes. This attractive plant has escaped from cultivation and become naturalized in wet habitats, resulting in the reduction or elimination of native species. It should be declared a noxious weed. A related species, winged loosestrife (*Lythrum alatum*), has simple or paired flowers in leaf axils and is native; it is not a problem.

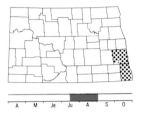

Richland County
August 1987

Kalm's lobelia   *Lobelia kalmii*

Stem erect, slender, usually unbranched, 1 to 3dm tall. Leaves linear-lanceolate to oblanceolate, 0.5 to 5cm long and 0.5 to 3mm wide, gradually reduced in size upward. Inflorescence a terminal raceme of 2 to 12 flowers, 1 per node. Flowers pale to dark blue, bilabiate, upper lip 2-lobed, lower lip 3-lobed; as the flowers open, the pedicel twists, inverting the flower so that the 2-lobed lip is uppermost. Occurs in fens and wet prairies.

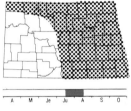

Mountrail County
August 1988

Blue cardinal flower   *Lobelia siphilitica*

Stems solitary, reaching 3 to 10dm in height. Leaves alternate, lanceolate, 2 to 15cm long, reduced in size upward. Flower cluster in a terminal raceme of 10 to 40 flowers, 1 flower per node; flower 1.5 to 3cm long, deep blue with a white stripe in the throat. Flower shape similar to that of Kalm's lobelia. Locally abundant in wet prairies and moist ditches.

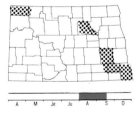

Ransom County
August 1987

110

Northern gentian   *Gentiana affinis*

Stems erect, usually clumped, 1 to 3.5dm tall. Leaves opposite, lanceolate, 1 to 3.5cm long, and 3 to 15mm wide. Inflorescence of several flowers in upper leaf axils. Flowers pale purple with whitish interior, 2 to 3cm long, funnel-shaped, 5-lobed with folds between the lobes. Uncommon, usually in wet prairies.

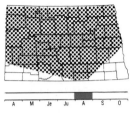

McHenry County
August 1988

Closed gentian   *Gentiana andrewsii*

Similar to the preceding but taller and with longer leaves (2 to 8cm long). Flowers in a dense, terminal cluster of 3 to 10 flowers, sometimes also with a few flowers in upper leaf axils. Petals purple and fused into a tube which is closed. Each flower resembling a tiny bottle, which gives rise to the common name "bottle gentian." Frequent in wet prairies and moist parts of upland prairies.

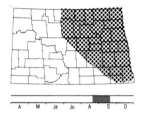

Ransom County
August 1987

Smooth blue aster   *Aster laevis*

Stems erect, branched, lower portion reddish, 3 to 10dm tall. Lower leaves petiolate, upper leaves sessile and clasping, greatly reduced in size near flowers; ovate to nearly linear, usually with entire margins. Inflorescence a paniculate cluster of several to many heads. Flowers showy, up to 2.5cm across, with 15 to 25 deep pink to purple ligules. Common on prairies and in open woods. There are 9 other species of asters with pinkish-bluish flowers in North Dakota.

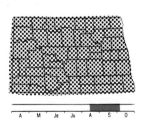

Pembina County
September 1987

112

Glossary

Achene—a small, dry, one-seeded fruit

Alternate—leaves occurring singly at a node and alternating on opposite sides of the stem

Areole—the spine-bearing area of a cactus

Auricle—an appendage shaped like an ear

Axil—the angle between a leaf or a branch and the stem on which it grows

Banner—the upper petal in the flower of a leguminous plant

Basal—located at the base of a plant or structure

Berry—a fleshy fruit containing several seeds

Biennial—living for two years

Bifid—two-cleft

Bilabiate—flower having two lips

Blade—the expanded terminal part of a leaf

Bract—a modified leaf, often below a flower or flower cluster

Calyx—the whorl of sepals

Campanulate—shaped like a bell

Capsule—a dry, dehiscent fruit of two or more carpels

Carpel—a simple pistil or one part of a compound pistil

Ciliate—fringed with marginal hairs

Compound umbel—umbellate flower in which each pedicel gives rise to an umbel; the flowers on each pedicel opening from outside inwards

Cordate—heart-shaped (leaf)

Corolla—the whorl of petals

Corymb—type of inflorescence that is similar to a raceme but with the flowers forming a flat or convex top and the outer flowers opening first

Cyme—type of inflorescence that is similar to a corymb but with the inner flowers opening first

Decumbent—base prostrate with ends erect

Decurrent—extending downward from point of insertion

Dehiscent—opening along preformed sutures

Dentate—toothed (leaf margin)

Disk—the central part of a flower head, containing tubular florets

Drupe—a fleshy fruit containing one seed enclosed in a shell

Exfoliating—flaking from surface

Floret—a single flower in a dense inflorescence, especially a head

Hastate—shaped like an arrowhead

Head—a dense cluster of partially or completely stalkless flowers which open from the outside inward

Hirsute—covered with stiff, long hairs

Hood—one part of the petals of milkweed flowers, the margins of which are incurved

Horn—an exserted appendage of the hood

Inflorescence—the arrangement of flowers on a plant

Involucre—one or more whorls of bracts beneath a flower or flower cluster

Involute—rolled inward on the upper side

Keel—the flower structure in leguminous plants formed by the union of the two lower petals

Lanceolate—elongate, narrow leaves that are broadest at the base and taper to the apex

Leaflet—one part of a compound leaf

Ligule—a strap-shaped structure, especially in the ray florets of heads

Linear—leaves that are long and narrow with parallel margins

Lip—one of the lobes in a two-lobed flower

Lobe—the rounded part of a leaf or petal

Node—the place on the stem where leaves, branches, or flowers arise

Oblanceolate—elongate, narrow leaves that are broadest near the apex and taper to the base

Obovate—egg-shaped leaves that are broadest near the apex

Ovate—egg-shaped leaves that are broadest near the base

Palmate—compound leaves with the leaflets arising from one point at the end of the petiole

Panicle—type of inflorescence that is an elongate, compound raceme, the flowers opening from the bottom of each stalk outwards

Pedicel—the stalk of a single flower

Peduncle—the stalk of a flower cluster; also applied to the stalk of the only flower of an inflorescence

Petal—one of the parts of the corolla of a flower

Petiole—the stalk of a leaf

Petiolate—having petioles

Pilose—covered with soft, thin hairs

Pinnate—compound leaves with the leaflets on both sides of the stalk

Pinnatifid—with pinnately-arranged lobes

Pistil—the seed-producing organ of a flower

Plicate—with lengthwise folds

Plumose—featherlike

Pome—a fleshy fruit formed from an inferior ovary with several locules

Prickle—small, weak, spiny outgrowths of the epidermis

Pubescence—hairs; usually short, soft hairs

Raceme—type of inflorescence in which the individual flowers are borne on pedicels on an elongate stalk and open from the bottom upwards

Ray—floret in the outer ring of florets in a head; usually with a ligule

Rosette—a cluster of leaves arranged in a circle

Scape—a leafless flowering stalk arising from the ground

Secund—arranged on one side

Sepal—one of the parts of the calyx of a flower

Serrate—leaf margin with forward pointing teeth

Sessile—lacking a stalk

Spadix—a dense spike of minute flowers

Spathe—a large leaf-like bract covering an inflorescence

Spike—type of inflorescence in which the individual flowers are sessile on an elongate stalk and open from the bottom upwards

Spine—a sharp-pointed, stiff projection from a stem

Spur—a hollow, tubular projection from a petal or sepal, often containing nectar

Stamen—the pollen-bearing organ of a flower

Stolen—a horizontal stem that roots at the nodes

Style—the elongated part of the pistil between the ovary and the stigma

Succulent—fleshy, juicy, and thickened

Tendril—a slender, twining structure used for support

Throat—the opening of a tubular corolla

Trifoliate—a compound leaf with three leaflets

Umbel—type of inflorescence in which the individual flowers are borne on pedicels that arise from a common point; the flowers open from the outside inward

Undulate—with a wavy margin

Villose—with long, soft hairs

Whorl—three or more parts arranged in a circle at a node

Winged—having a thin extension of an organ

References

The following publications either contain references to wildflowers occurring in North Dakota or are useful in identifying the species of plants known to occur in the state.

Great Plains Flora Association. 1977. *Atlas of the Flora of the Great Plains.* Ames, IA. Iowa State University Press.

Great Plains Flora Association. 1986. *Flora of the Great Plains.* Lawrence, KS. University Press of Kansas.

Rydberg, P. A. 1932. *Flora of the Prairies and Plains of Central North America.* New York, NY. New York Botanical Garden.

Staudinger, J. D. 1967. *Wild Flowers of Theodore Roosevelt National Memorial Park.* Medora, ND. Theodore Roosevelt Nature and History Association.

Stevens, O. A. 1933. *Wild Flowers of North Dakota.* North Dakota Agricultural College, Agricultural Experiment Station, Bulletin 269.

Stevens, O. A. 1950. *Handbook of North Dakota Plants.* Fargo, ND. North Dakota Institute for Regional Studies.

Van Bruggen, T. 1983. *Wildflowers, Grasses and Other Plants of the Northern Plains and Black Hills.* Interior, SD. Badlands Natural History Association.

Vance, F. R., J. R. Jowsey, and J. S. McLean. 1984. *Wildflowers of the Northern Great Plains.* Minneapolis, MN. University of Minnesota Press.

Index to Scientific Names

Opuntia polyacantha	54	Smilacina stellata	14
Oxalis stricta	52	Solanum rostratum	58
Oxytropis campestris	16	Solidago gigantea	64
lambertii	98	ptarmicoides	38
Penstemon albidus	18	rigida	64
eriantherus	100	Sonchus arvensis	60
gracilis	100	oleraceus	60
Phlox hoodii	8	Sphaeralcea coccinea	72
Physostegia parviflora	90	Spiranthes cernua	34
Polygala alba	18	Spirea alba	28
Polygonatum biflorum	54	Symphoricarpos occidentalis	80
Polygonum amphibium	84	Teucrium canadense	86
convolvulus	32	Thalictrum venulosum	26
Potentilla anserina	50	Thermopsis rhombifolia	42
arguta	28	Townsendia exscapa	22
Prenanthes alba	38	Tradescantia bracteata	98
Prunus virginiana	10	Tragopogon dubius	46
Psoralea argophylla	104	Trillium cernuum	8
Pyrola elliptica	30	Verbena hastata	108
Ranunculus flabellaris	56	stricta	108
hispidus	44	Vernonia fasciculata	106
Ratibida columnifera	58	Veronica americana	96
Rosa acicularis	78	Viburnum opulus	10
arkansana	78	Vicia americana	74
Rudbeckia hirta	56	Viola canadensis	12
laciniata	70	pratincola	94
Sagittaria cuneata	34	pubescens	42
Scutellaria galericulata	102	Yucca glauca	30
Senecio canus	48	Zigadenus elegans	24
Silene noctiflora	26	Zizia aptera	44
Sisyrinchium montanum	94		

Index to Common Names

Acknowledgments

This book would not have been possible without the cooperation and assistance of a number of individuals. Several landowners permitted me access to the natural areas under their control. In particular, I appreciate the cooperation of Roland and Norma Pullen of Beach for study on their ranch near Sentinel Butte, Suzette Bieri and Mike Jacobs of Grand Forks for inviting me to their farm near Blaisdell, and Roland and the late Lois Young for access to the Red River Valley woods adjacent to their home south of Grand Forks.

Identification of plants is not as easy as it may seem to readers of this book. I have been fortunate to have as a faculty colleague a systematist, John LaDuke. He has patiently checked specimens that I collected, often correcting my mistaken identifications. However, because many of the photographs were taken before John joined the faculty and some of the voucher specimens were discarded, I take full responsibility for the identifications in this book.

The manuscript for this book has been prepared while I have been on developmental leave from the University of North Dakota. Financial support in the form of a Developmental Leave Supplement from the Office of Instructional Development has contributed to the preparation of the final manuscript.

I thank Nikki R. Seabloom of *The Prairie Naturalist* for proofreading the manuscript, Ken Dorscher of the North Dakota Geological Survey for drawing Figure 1, Phyllis Erickson of the Academic Media Center, University of North Dakota, for drawing Figure 3, and David H. Vorland, Executive Assistant to the President, University of North Dakota, for arranging funds to cover part of the publication costs.

The Author

Paul B. Kannowski is a member of the faculty of the Biology Department at the University of North Dakota, which he joined in 1957 after completing his Ph. D. degree at the University of Michigan and teaching for a year at Bowling Green State University in Ohio. During his tenure at the University of North Dakota he has served twice as chair of the Biology Department, 1963-70 and 1982-88. He also served as Director of the Institute for Ecological Studies at the University from 1965 to 1981. Professor Kannowski's research has centered primarily on the behavior and ecology of ants, which he has carried out in various regions of the United States and in Mexico, Costa Rica, and Panama. He has been honored with election in 1963 as a Fellow of the American Association for the Advancement of Science and in 1979 as a Fellow of the Explorers Club. In 1988 he received the Professional Award of the Central Mountains and Plains Section of The Wildlife Society. In addition to his University responsibilities, Dr. Kannowski has been the editor of *The Prairie Naturalist*, quarterly journal of Great Plains ecology and natural history, since its founding in 1968.

Copies of Photographs

Enlargements suitable for framing of the photographs in this book are available for purchase. Reproductions 7 inches by 10 inches cost $20.00 each; those 10 inches by 14 inches cost $25.00 each, including sales tax and postage. Other sizes may be special ordered.

Also available are notecards containing photographs of several of the flowers. These are packaged in groups of ten cards and matching linen envelopes; each package contains cards representing four different flowers. These cards are available at a cost of $7.00 per package including sales tax and postage. These cards are also available at certain bookstores and gift shops in North Dakota.

All proceeds from the sale of these items and this book will be deposited in a Biology Department account to cover printing expenses and to support field research on North Dakota fauna and flora. Orders may be sent to Wildflowers, Department of Biology, University of North Dakota, Grand Forks, ND 58202-8238.

Notes

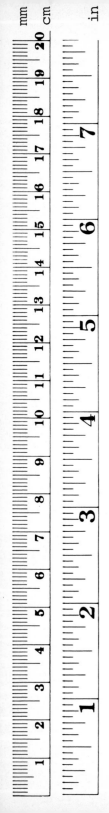